Taste the Youth Ministry
Cultivating Organic Faith in Korean American Youth Ministry

Praise Presbyterian Church
15 Cedar Grove Lane Somerset New Jersey 08873 www.praiseyouth.com

Praise youth
Taste the Truth

Joo Whang
2009

Contents

FORWARD

CHAPTER ONE
    YOUTH...PASTOR?   7

CHAPTER TWO
    CULTIVATING ORGANIC FAITH   20

CHAPTER THREE
    THE YOUTH MINISTRY OF MOSES   26
        THE FIVE DEUTERONOMIC CATECHETICAL PRINCIPLES

CHAPTER FOUR
    THE STAYING POWER OF *JEONG*   47

CHAPTER FIVE
    PRACTICAL TOOLS   69
        Ministry Standards for Youth Pastors &
        Teaching Tools for the First Days of Ministry

CHAPTER SIX
    CONCLUSION: REMEMBERING MOSES   93

BIBLIOGRAPHY

FORWARD

I have never felt more out of place or at a loss as the first time I stepped into Praise Presbyterian Church. I was as green as a newly hired youth pastor could be. And to add to my worries, this was my first experience with a Korean American youth ministry. The youth that are still around to remember those first trial-filled months still laugh at my initial attempts at using chopsticks and the way I scrunched up my nose after being force-fed a mouthful of Kimchi. I look back on those months (they seem so long ago now) with a certain fondness—the fondness one has for a difficult mission accomplished, or a rough road safely navigated. With the clear vision of hindsight, I can confidently say that I wish I had known the things I read in this book back then.

I felt a bit like I was reading a biography of my own first year of ministry at Praise Youth as I traversed these pages. All the difficulties Pastor Joo describes for new *jundosas*—these were my difficulties. Even though I think I skipped Pastor Joo's "Fantasy" stage that he lists in "The Four Stages of *Jundosa*," I am certainly familiar with the "Survival" stage. And, hopefully, I have now begun to move on to "Mastery." No matter where I am now, though, I can only imagine how helpful it would have been to have had this introduction to Korean American ministry (and youth ministry, in general) when I was first starting out. I don't know if it would have made those first months any easier. But in the same way that one can take the first step of a hard journey more confidently with a map in hand, the guidance offered here for first-time youth pastors is a powerful tool for preparation.

In addition to the solid, practical advice, I love Pastor Joo's inclusion of a truly Biblical model for youth ministers. I had never thought about Moses as a youth pastor before. But now I can just imagine going out for coffee with the revered patriarch, chatting about those...special students, thinking up new ministry activities, and asking how the Israelites did at that last game of "Chubby

Bunny!" As this book mentions, it is difficult to find good models for youth ministry in the Bible. Adolescence is a modern concept that simply did not exist with Abraham, David, or the Apostles. Yet God's passion for our younger generations is clear. Youth ministry has tended to be more and more influenced by secular methodologies and technologies. And there are certainly valuable lessons and tools to be found there. But this is why I think Pastor Joo's exegetical approach is so important. We need a Biblical vantage point to best judge the secular methods we are considering to adopt.

I think the absolute best advice that can be offered to any new youth pastor can be found in the conclusion of this book: "In God's everlasting mo-jeong, we must never stop praying for our youth. Just like Christ never ceases to pray for all of us, let us never cease to pray for our youth members and their families until we literally see God face to face." Let me only add my own prayer to this: I pray and have faith that God will provide among our youth today the leaders for the church tomorrow—leaders like Moses, who will continue to pass on the good news of our Lord Jesus Christ.

Pastor Brian White
Director of Praise Youth Ministry
December 2009

CHAPTER ONE

Youth...
Pastor?

"These are the commands, decrees and laws the LORD your God directed me to teach you to observe in the land that you are crossing the Jordan to possess, so that you and your children and your children's children may fear the Lord your God all the days of your life, and keep all his decrees and his commandments...so that your days may be long" (Deut 6:1-2).

"Joshua son of Nun, the servant of the LORD died at the age of a hundred and ten. And they buried him in the land of his inheritance, at Timnath Heres in the hill country of Ephraim, north of Mount Gaash. After that whole generation had been gathered to their fathers, another generation grew up, who knew neither the LORD nor what he had done for Israel. Then the Israelites did evil in the eyes of the LORD and served the Baals." (Judges 2:8-11).

I don't get it! What had happened here? In Deuteronomy, Moses taught the next generation, Joshua's generation, very intensively about the essential life lesson of loving the LORD their God with all their heart and with all their soul and with all their strength. Furthermore, Joshua's generation witnessed the old generation's mistrust of God in the wilderness, and thus they seemed to receive a crucial faith lesson from the older generations. According to Judges 2, however, Joshua's generation failed to pass on their faith to their children. Why? What went wrong? Or a more urgent and applicable question to Korean-American churches for today would be, "What about us, aren't we also failing to pass on the faith to the next generation?" The warning seems very clear to Korean-American (KA) churches today: a faithful community seems always one generation away from ceasing. The membership growth rate of KA churches or the number of church buildings cannot guarantee the spiritual well-being of the next generation among the KA community. It is time to seriously reform our attitudes about youth ministry (including children's ministry) in KA churches, since the concern of passing the faith to the younger generation is at the heart of youth ministry. The call of faithfully educating "who the LORD is and what the LORD has done" (Judges 2:10) to the younger generation is not only given to Moses or Joshua, but also to youth pastors of today. It is youth pastors' responsibility to passionately teach "who the LORD is and what the LORD has done" to the next generation, so their "children's children may fear the LORD."

Korean-Americans of Today

The time has shifted. Many Korean immigrants in the United States have crossed their "Red Sea," finishing their journey in the "wilderness" to their "Promised Land" of the American Dream. There are still groups of recent immigrants with low education or lack of economic resources who struggle to achieve their dreams. The overall Korean immigrant society, however, achieved their financial goal in this success-driven society. For the result of such an effort, their second-generation children became the primary beneficiaries of their parents' hard work. According to the U.S. Census 2000, the living conditions for KA children (the parents' average income, house/rental conditions, number of automobiles, etc.) are above the overall American average.[1] The success of the first-generation immigrants directly influenced their ethnic churches as well. Many KA churches are now paying much more attention to the spiritual education for the younger generations. In some highly populated areas like Los Angeles and New York, the third-generation KAs are even becoming a notable ministry group in their churches.[2] With a long immigrant history in the States, KA people seem to be no longer a nomadic people in this land. The parent generations' arduous labors allowed their children to cross the "Jordan River" to the final destination of the prosperous "Promised Land."

At the heart of this remarkable immigrant establishment is the Korean immigrant church, which played a crucial role for its community as a spiritual and emotional shelter. Similar to the Puritans, the first-generation Korean immigrants regularly gathered together to pray and worship when they first arrived to this land. In the midst of harsh immigrant life, the community of faith offered a place of comfort and peace. Along with them came their children. Similar to Joshua's generation, the second-generation witnessed their parents' spirituality (both good and bad) in the "wilderness" of immigrant life. Whether the younger generation wanted or not, through their parents, the children became a part of the church community, at least on Sunday mornings.

In many cases, however, the children or youth ministries in Korean churches were treated as a secondary concern or, perhaps, a

---

[1] According to the U.S. Census Bureau, the median family income for Korean American family is $60,600, compared to $55,832 for the overall U.S. families. See U.S. Census Bureau for other information. (http://www.census.gov)

[2] Youngnak Church of L.A., one of the biggest KA churches in the States has a membership of 5,000 1st generation Korean adult members (KM) and about 2,000 2nd generation or English speaking adult members (EM). The 3rd generation KA, the children of Youngnak EM members is also growing (www.youngnak.com). Another notable church is Praise Presbyterian Church in New Jersey. Usually, KA churches have one education department (children and youth church) for both children from 1st and 2nd generation congregations. But Praise church has two different education departments. Currently about 300 children and youth are the 2nd generation children which belong to KC (Korean Congregation) and 40 children and youth are the 3rd generation children in EC (English Congregation). The presence of the third generation Korean-Americans are apparent throughout the KA churches.

"minor league" in their churches. It is true that the overall condition of the spiritual education for the second and third generation has been improved greatly. This effort, however, is not sufficient since the so called "silent-exodus" happened in many KA churches, where majority of the second generation believers have left the church after the high school.[3] The number of full-time ministry job postings for children or youth ministry at Korean-American Christian search engines further adds the concern. [4] According to these search engines, a KA church usually seeks a full-time position for a senior pastor, associate pastor, or English Ministry (EM) pastor. On the contrary, one may easily find many available "part-time" positions for children's and youth ministries within the ministry job postings. One of the reasons for this phenomenon is a lack of resources (both money and pastors) among KA churches. The core reason, however, lies somewhere else.

Academically-Centered Parents

For many KA parents, their primary concern for their children is not spiritual education, but academic education so that their kids may continue or accomplish parents' American Dream. With an exceptional value of a higher education, the parent's effort to provide the best education to their child usually starts with living in a good school district. The first generation Korean parents call that *hakgoon*, literally a school district. Parents in a KA church love to talk about good *hakgoons* with other parents because it is their prime concern for their children. Their financial goal is not only to purchase a good house, but a good house in a good *hakgoon*. Deep inside of Korean mentality, receiving a good education is the starting point to be prosperous in the future for the young

---

[3] Kwon, Kim, and Warner., ed. *Korean Americans and Their Religions: Pilgrims and Missionaries from a Different Shore*, 141.
[4] Three biggest Christian related search engines are The Korean Christian Mission USA (www.kcmusa.com), The Christian Herald USA (www.christianherald.com), and Korean-American Ministry Resources (www.kamr.org).

generation. Good education during elementary school leads a child to be academically successful in junior and senior high school, which then leads him/her to a prestigious college. Starting with the toddler years, it seems as if entering one of the prestigious colleges is the main goal of a child's education. Therefore, looking for a good *hakgoon* for their children is one of the most crucial parenting jobs for many KA parents. The church for these academically-oriented parents, then, becomes an "extracurricular activity" center or a "spiritual guidance for academics" place for their children.

The weekly schedule for many KA teenagers in these days perhaps confirms my concern. Most teenagers in Korean cultures (both in Korea and America) are not free after their daily school education. Their daily life is full of extra curricular activities, such as music and sports lessons so they may add a few more impressive lines in their resume for college. Moreover, students often receive academic tutoring to raise their G.P.A. and SAT scores. All these means of extra education are very costly to the parents. At some time in Korean history, it became a common standard among Korean culture to consider spending lots of money on children's education a virtue, rather than a luxury or burden. The parents' concern for providing the best education to their children is not a problematic issue since it is a natural part of parenting. Unfortunately, however, academic education without "the fear of the LORD" forces many of our youth members to only be multi-talented elites in a success-driven society. There is no room for spiritual education in this busy teenager's life. It seems "free" spiritual education through a youth ministry comes last in many parents' agenda. I wonder about the generation after this young generation. Will they know who the LORD is and what the LORD has done for them?

In his honest daily journal, Henri J. M. Nouwen addresses a similar concern for his people. While visiting his homeland, Holland, Nouwen notes:

> The most remarkable thing about Holland is its prosperity… The country feels very self-satisfied.

> There is not much space left, inside or outside, to be with God and God alone. It is hard to explain why Holland changed from a very pious to a very secular country in one generation. Many reasons can be given. But it seems to me… their captivating prosperity is one of the more obvious reasons. People are just very busy-eating, drinking, and going places… Paul van Vliet, a well-known Dutch comedian, used, as one of the themes in his Christmas TV show, "We are smart but very distracted." Indeed, we know and understand what we most need, but we just don't get around to it, since we are so busy playing with our toys. There is too much to play with! No real time to grow up and do the necessary thing: "Love God and each other."[5]

The seriousness of Nouwen's concern for his people continues in the next journal entry. After realizing that none of his family members, except his six-year-old niece, are willing to go with Nouwen to celebrate the Eucharist in the nearby parish church on New Year's Eve, Nouwen questions, "I keep wondering how, in one generation, such a pious family could lose so completely its connection with God and God's church."[6] I am afraid to confess that I see a similar pattern in Korea and the Korean-American community in these days. The most remarkable thing about Korea is its prosperity compared to its painful history during the early 20th century. Similar to Korean economic history, Korean immigrants in America also established their amazing affluence in a short time. The symptoms of such result seem to follow Nouwen's concern as well.

Gradually, the KA community too is beginning to feel "very self-satisfied" through the prosperity, yet the people seem very distracted. Or more accurately, our highly competitive adolescents

---

[5] Henri Nouwen, *The Road to Daybreak: A Spiritual Journey*, 108.
[6] Ibid., 110.

are becoming more a "smart but very distracted" people in this society. Both the society and the parents are failing to offer "real time to grow up and do the necessary thing: Love God and each other."

It seems almost impossible for us young and inexperienced "youth pastors" to convince the "academically-oriented" first generation parents that "the fear of the LORD is [*really*] the beginning of knowledge" (Prov. 1:7). Quite often, the public school teachers' advice is valued more highly than the youth pastors' regarding the future of the child. It is unfortunate, but my two-year high school teaching experience convinced me that Korean parents pay more attention to academic teachers than spiritual teachers. In the case of ethical or moral problems of a child, the parents seem to seek help from his/her youth pastor. But even in that situation, the concern of the parents is mostly about the child's G.P.A., not the possible broken relationship with God. Many parents seem to regularly monitor their children's academic life through G.P.A. , but not the spiritual life.

Youth Pastors and KA Churches

I cannot, however, only blame the parents for the "silent exodus" phenomenon. Youth pastors are also responsible for not treating the faith seriously and urgently enough to our youth members and to their parents. Although I strongly believe that the parents are still the most influential spiritual leaders for their children, the KA churches and their youth pastors also needs to share the holy burdens of the parents. The major problem that I see from the parents is that many parents do not know how to educate their children spiritually, or perhaps they do not consider this role of being a spiritual teacher as part of their parenthood. This is why many of them consider the youth pastors as the source of their children's spiritual education. The youth pastors of these parents, therefore, must include the parents and family ministry in the youth program. The youth ministry boundary, thus, needs to extend its normal boundary of membership (usually consisting of youth members, adult volunteers, and a youth pastor) by including parents in our ministry. Parents of a youth member must have their role in youth ministry, so the spiritual education can continue during the weekdays in their family as well.

Ron Taffel, a psychologist and counselor of adolescents, offers a crucial insight: "one of my central goals is to help teens stop believing that parents or other responsible adults can never understand, that real talk is reserved only for other kids."[7] He continues, "I hope teens will talk more to their parents—so that they will need to talk less to me."[8] The "real talk" of spiritual conversation is a bit different since youth members consider their youth pastor as the spiritual leader, but the role of the parents seems to follow the similar pattern. Many teens of today believe that the "real talk" of spirituality does not belong to their parents. As a result, the youth pastors are often perceived as the only spiritual counselor of their choice. The lesson behind such challenge is not that to prohibit the youth members to conduct the "real talk" with the youth pastors, but to encourage both parents and their children to converse with each other about their spiritual lives. Youth pastors must have a similar hope of Taffel in our ministry. Having lots of meaningful spiritual conversations with youth members does not make the minister a successful youth pastor if the parents have no room in the youth member's spiritual life. Rather, the youth pastors need to encourage parents to become the life-long spiritual conversation partner to their children so the youth can talk to their parents more than to their youth pastors.

The unique reality of KA churches adds another complex issue to youth ministry. The most common problem among KA churches is the lack of children and youth pastors. A recent article from the Los Angeles Times addressed the concern of the lack of second generation pastors among Asian Americans. It reports that attendance of Asian seminarians has decreased significantly in the

---

[7] Ron Taffel, *Breaking Through to Teens*. 76.
[8] Ibid., 77.

past ten years.⁹ A KA church that lacks children or a youth pastor, therefore, has no option but to hire any available KA seminarian. In this desperate church setting, three main problems have started to appear in Korean-American churches.

1) "The part-time job" for inexperienced *jundosa*

> The majority of Korean American churches even hire first year-seminarians as their part-time children or youth ministers because the church desperately needs someone to take care of the children and youth. Seminarians in a KA church are called *Jundosa* (literally "Evangelist"), which is the official title for children/youth pastor before ordination. Even if the person has no prior ministry experience, he/she becomes *Jundosa* for the ministry. The status of *Jundosa* is quite different from an intern because *Jundosa* is in charge of the ministry. Quite often, an inexperienced *Jundosa* is expected to lead the whole ministry successfully.

2) Too much responsibility without a proper support.

> The churches' expectation from the *jundosa* is very high. Quite often, the first generation senior pastors expect their *jundosa*s to do more work (than the usual seminary field education requirements) because they themselves had extremely intensive intern experiences in their seminary years in Korea. The first generation pastors' *jundosa* experience at Korean seminaries is radically different from

---

[9] "Recruiting Asian American seminarians is "a major challenge," said Fumitaka Matsuoka, former dean of the Pacific School of Religion in Berkeley. "We have generous financial aid, but even with that, it's hard." Matsuoka said only three or four Asian American students are enrolled at his seminary, a stone's throw from UC Berkeley, where 43% of students are Asian American. "The discrepancy is incredible," he said. At Princeton Theological Seminary in New Jersey, Asian American students number about 50 — down from more than 100 in the 1990s, according to the Rev. Sang Hyun Lee, a professor of systematic theology and director of the seminary's Asian American program" (www.latimes.com/news/local/la-me-beliefs3mar03,1,1318985,full.story).

American ones. Korean seminary education systems in Korea demand far more ministry services than the American education. "Extra hard work" is expected among Korean seminarians in Korea because of the high competition. Many of these "part-timers" have no prior experience of running ministry as a leader/pastor. Moreover, except in the mega church settings, there is literally no adequate supervisor (who knows the youth ministry) to support the *jundosa*. As a result, both youth group and the youth worker suffer together. The lack of support from the church leads youth workers to burn out quickly and to leave the ministry within one or two years.

3) Problem of burnout

It seems that many of the seminarians leave their first ministry (usually children or youth ministry) as soon as they graduate from their seminary. There are two major reasons for leaving the ministry. The first reason is that they need a full time position for their living but not many churches can offer full time position for youth and children's ministry. Thus, many KA seminarians choose other ministries over the youth ministry. The second reason is that they are "burned out" from doing the youth or children's ministry. Through the part-time *jundosa* experience, which is very demanding, many of the young seminarians decide to stay away from the ministry.

It is truly unfortunate that there are not many full time positions available for youth or children's ministry. The even more poignant phenomena is that there are not many future pastors who want to be a youth or children's pastor due to their "burn out" experiences during the seminary years. I believe that the biggest victim of the above problems is not youth workers, but youth members who live in this unfortunate church dynamic. It is a harsh reality of the KA churches, but it is not impossible to change.

Passing On Faith to the Next Generation

In the midst of the current situation, the warning from Judges 2:10 cannot be ignored: the new generation in the Promised Land "knew neither the LORD nor what he had done for Israel" (Jud. 2:11). I believe this warning directly applies to KA churches today. Statistically, Korean churches in the United States are considered one of the fastest growing congregations.[10] However, membership growth cannot guarantee the continuation of the next generations' faith in Christ. The number of Israelites who experienced Yahweh's awesome miracles was huge, yet the generation failed to pass on their faith in God to their descendants.

If youth pastors do not have the power to change the whole dynamics of the KA churches, then youth pastors must start the "reformation" process in their youth group. Youth pastors in the KA church settings have spent by far too much time searching for the best youth ministry curriculum to satisfy the need of the current KA cultural conditions. Developing or creating a curriculum of a new paradigm or a new program in youth ministry is needed, but it is not absolutely necessary for passing on the faith. That is not the most urgent concern for the KA churches today. The most necessary and significant curriculum that the church need today is a faithful youth pastor. Youth ministers are *the* curriculum for youth ministry. If youth pastors do not show a burning passion for Christ, the youth members will not live their lives passionately for Christ as well. It is true for both youth pastors and their observers, "if Jesus isn't worth dying for, he isn't worth living for, either."[11]

The metaphor of "gardening" as an expression of ministry offers a helpful picture of my thesis. I would like to suggest this "gardening" image for youth ministry of today. Youth pastors are like the gardeners who are called to tend the ground and cultivate

---

[10] According to PCUSA Church Growth Statistics of 2004, Korean-American churches in PCUSA are considered one of the fastest growth churches (http://www.pcusa.org/korean/pdf/2005-statistics.pdf). The national Council of the Churches also reported the similar results (http://www.electronicchurch.org/2002/NCC_members.htm).
[11] Kenda Dean, *Practicing Passion*, 32.

God's garden of youth ministry. The gardener in this garden must not forget that God is the one who provides the ground, the water, the light, and the seed. Weather the fruits will yield or not wholly depends on God. As a gardener, however, we are called to faithfully cultivate the garden so the seeds can receive nutritious and healthy faith. In my experience, God does not demand a mass production through our cultivation. In that sense, God prefers us to cultivate "organic" fruits, which are handled carefully with our own hands without any genetic reproduction tricks.[12]

I find that Moses' youth ministry in Deuteronomy as the helpful cultivation model for youth pastors of today. The book of Deuteronomy, as the catechism of book for the younger generation, offers urgent message of cultivating the organic faith to the contemporary youth. Along with Moses' cultivation manual, I realize that Korean Americans need to acquire their own cultural gardening tool since their cultivating ground (KA church setting) is uniquely different than the other cultural grounds. Using the Korean concept of *jeong* (which means love, attachment, affection and more) as the next gardening tool, I will explain how this concept and practice of *jeong* can help KA youth pastors to become sensitive gardeners for their ground. Finally, I find the theology of the Cross the necessary gardening tool to complement the possible misuse of the *jeong* in the KA context. The Cross will teach us that the *jeong* is a cultural human tool that can be abused in a wrong way.

---

[12] *Wikipedia* offers helpful definition of organic food. It explains, "Organic food is produced according to certain legally regulated standards. For crops, it means they were grown without the use of conventional pesticides, artificial fertilizers or sewage sludge, and that they were processed without ionizing radiation or food additives. For animals, it means they were reared without the routine use of antibiotics and without the use of growth hormones. Also, at all levels, organic food is produced without the use of genetically modified organisms" (http://en.wikipedia.org/wiki/Organic_food). In a similar way, I used the word "organic" on faith to convey the quality of the faith teaching which is not geared towards fast growth or massive amount of abundant spiritual life of a teenager. As Reformed theology teaches, the Christian faith is the gift of God. Just like a seed, faith grows. The organic faith, therefore, concerns the process of such growth. With highly regulated standards, this faith in our youth members must be treated carefully.

The effect of *jeong* can only be maximized with the message of the Cross.

Korean immigrant churches are about to cross the Jordan River. Although all of the current conditions greatly challenge "part-time" or "full-time" youth pastors, it is still youth pastors who need to cultivate the ground. As many social psychologists confirm, the surrounding culture and community play a critical role in identity formation of a youth. A healthy spiritual identity formation also requires a deeply caring and relational community of faith that encourages exploration of faith. Youth pastors can provide such community with organic faith. Apostle Paul further encourages, "[we, who are] less than the least of all God's holy people, have been entrusted with this special grace, of proclaiming to the Gentiles the unfathomable treasure of Christ and of throwing light on the inner workings of the mystery kept hidden through all the ages in God, the Creator of everything" (Eph. 3:8-9). More than ever, it is time for youth pastors to cultivate the ground by boldly proclaiming "the unfathomable riches of Christ" to youth members.

CHAPTER TWO

CULTIVATING
ORGANIC FAITH

> *During evening prayer we sang simple songs, we listened to Danny, one of the handicapped men from Cork, ... Danny said, "I love you, Jesus. I do not reject you even when I get nervous once in a while... even when I get confused. I love you with my arms, my legs, my head, my heart; I love you and I do not reject you, Jesus. I know that you love me, that you love me so much. I love you too, Jesus." As he prayed I looked at his beautiful, gentle face and saw without any veil or cover his agony as well as his love. Who would not respond to a prayer like that?*[13]

This prayer of Danny stopped me from reading Henri Nouwen's daily journal, *The Road to Daybreak*, for a moment to reflect on my prayer life. As a youth pastor at my church or even as

---

[13] Nouwen, *The Road to Daybreak: A Spiritual Journey*, 11.

a seminarian for the past three years, I wondered how often I had offered a prayer like Danny's. Indeed Nouwen's expression is quite true: "Who would not respond to a prayer like that?" While I was diving into a short time of confession, my contrite heart turned to a hopeful vision for my youth members. As I followed Danny's prayer and experienced a time of solitude with my love Jesus Christ, I started to imagine my youth members praying like Danny in our youth group meetings. It would be every youth pastor's thrilling dream to see his/her adolescents come and pray like Danny at their youth groups. That is my dream as well, to see every one of my youth members confessing their love to Jesus out loud with a "beautiful and gentle" face. That seems to be the sign of the organic faith.

One of the major goals for youth ministry is to nurture youth with the healthiest possible organic faith to follow Jesus Christ completely, so they may also pass on their faith to the generation after them. The organic faith means the highest quality of the theological teaching for each individual, and it never attempts to produce fruits of a teenager's spiritual life either quickly or massively through human techniques. The organic faith is absolutely rooted in the Scriptures and the Holy Spirit. It comes from God, through the Scriptures, with the guidance of the Holy Spirit. The goal of providing the organic faith is not to build our youth ministry as one of the fastest and biggest youth programs so other churches can imitate such our techniques. Rather its goal is to provide nutritious faith-education to each adolescent so each soul can genuinely fall in love with Christ. It seems Danny has been receiving such an organic faith from his community. I cannot wait to see our youth confessing their genuine love to Jesus with a "beautiful and gentle" prayer face.

The Whole Food Market

The marketing of the Whole Food Market grocery store helps me to relate the importance of nurturing healthy food for our body and healthy faith for our soul. This "organic" food market is now the world's leading retailer of natural and organic foods in today's mass production world. The price is a bit expensive, but I became a fan of this market because of its quality and flavor. It has now become common sense that organic foods are healthier than mass produced non-organic items, but people do not know the difference in quality unless they actually taste it for themselves.

Teaching faith to youth requires a similar concept of healthiness. Unless adolescents taste the goodness of genuine organic faith in a youth group, they will simply be comfortable with mass produced "Moralistic Therapeutic" faith that promotes being happy and feeling good about oneself as the central goal of life.[14] Similar to the food industry, our churches have been busy "feeding," or hastily evangelizing, people with mass-produced curricula of faith. It is easier and faster to promote such a faith to the "customers" of today's Christians who seem to consider the church as "the spiritual marketplace."[15] As a result, the body of the church has grown bigger and fatter, but with serious detriment to its spirituality and theology. The lack of basic knowledge about the Bible and Christian theology among adolescents in our churches are the main symptoms.

Youth ministers now must reflect on the quality and intention of theological education in their youth ministry. Is the youth ministry nurturing the healthiest possible spiritual food to the teenagers? Or are youth programs of today attempting to feed the quick and easy junk faith to attract more hungry adolescents? The organic faith promotes the balanced teaching of Jesus Christ in his life, death, and resurrection. It teaches both life and death, suffering and healing, as well as death and resurrection of our life through

---

[14] Christian Smith and Melinda Denton use the phrase "Moralistic Therapeutic Deism" to explain the de facto dominant religions among contemporary U.S. teenagers. They offer five common beliefs of "Moralistic Therapeutic Deists": "1) A God exists who created and orders the world and watches over human life on earth. 2) God wants people to be good, nice, and fair to each other, as taught in the Bible and YHWH most world religions. 3) The central goal of life is to be happy and to feel good about oneself. 4) God does not need to be particularly involved in one's life except when God is needed to resolve a problem. 5) Good people go to heaven when they die." (Smith and Denton, *Soul Searching: The Religious and Spiritual Lives of American Teenagers*, 162-163)

[15] Wade C. Roof, *Spiritual Market Place*.

Jesus Christ. It does not promote cheap grace, but the suffering God who offered costly love. Furthermore, similar to the organic food items, the organic faith proudly recognizes and labels where it came from and how it has been produced. The organic faith comes from God, therefore, the quality is excellent. We need to promote this healthy faith to the youth.

The connecting goal of providing (or teaching) the whole faith to youth is to encourage a lifetime journey with Christ so they may also pass on the organic faith to the next generation. Youth pastors cannot nurture any youth member for a lifetime. Therefore, they must not only feed youth members, but discipline them to nurture themselves for the rest of their lives. Youth pastors must offer both fish and fishing skills to youth, so they may also taste and transfer the faith to the next generation. In response, adolescents will learn that their role as followers of Christ includes not only experiencing God on a personal level, but having absolute responsibility for passing on the faith to the next generation. Following Christ must not stop at high school graduation day. It has to be a process, since "Jesus is in the process of coming."[16]

The mass production of food through today's advanced scientific technology offers good food at a cheap price. In order to satisfy the growing human population, the mass production of food is necessary. This phenomenon has caused companies like the Whole Foods Market to advertise naturally grown, healthy "organic" foods to those who can afford them. Organic foods offer genuine nutrition to those who are concerned about their physical health. These kinds of healthy foods are even more appealing to parents who wish to provide the best nutrition for their kids. The following philosophy of the Whole Food Market's company addresses such parents' concern,

> Our motto — Whole Foods, Whole People, Whole Planet — emphasizes that our vision reaches far beyond just being a food retailer… Our goal is to sell the highest quality products that also offer high

---

[16] Jurgen Moltmann, *In the End-The beginning: The Life of Hope*, 89.

> value for our customers... Our product quality standards focus on ingredients, freshness, taste, nutritive value, safety and/or appearance... Whole Foods Market's vision of a sustainable future means our children and grandchildren will be living in a world that values human creativity, diversity, and individual choice.[17]

The Whole Foods Market's vision of "sustainable future," the better world for "our children and grandchildren" makes me believe this company is more than a food retailer. It almost sounds like a religious group that worships healthiness through healthy food. The motto of the company also conveys their ambition for expanding the kingdom of healthiness, starting with healthy food, then healthy people, and finally the whole world. "The whole food" makes people healthy and, in response, "the whole people" then will keep the planet healthy. In order to accomplish these goals, customers must pay a little more money for their organic products. It is pricy, but it is worth it.

It is every parent's prayer for his/her children to grow healthy and strong. But what about spiritual well-being for our children and grandchildren? Of course the spiritual realm is radically different from the tangible physical world. Moreover, we must not be confused about our faith by treating it as a "product" to advertise and sell in our advertisement-oriented capitalist society. Faith is radically different from food. The goal that I see, however, is very similar: to provide a healthy life for people and their children.

The book of Deuteronomy had a similar concern for their children. As Patrick D. Miller correctly points out in his Deuteronomy commentary, "no book of the Bible manifests a greater concern for the transmission of the faith to the next

---

[17] The Philosophy of the Whole Food Markets. 2004. Whole Food Market Company Information. 23 December 2006 <
http://www.wholefoodsmarket.com/company/philosophy.html>

generation."[18] Moses, who has seen and tasted the "unhealthy" faith of his generation in the desert for forty years, is desperate to teach the next generation what it means to love YHWH wholeheartedly. Moses' role in this book therefore is more than a law-giver or a leader of the Israelites, but a teacher and a youth pastor who wishes to deliver the whole faith to the younger generation. Deuteronomy 6:1-2 clearly states Moses' goal of teaching organic faith in his youth ministry, "so that you and your children and your children's children may fear the Lord your God all the days of your life, and keep all his decrees and his commandments…so that your days may be long" (Deut. 6:2). It is not only healthy food that promotes a "long life," but we need the healthy faith as well.

---

[18] Patrick D. Miller, *Deuteronomy, Interpretation, A Bible Commentary for Teaching and Preaching*, viii.

CHAPTER THREE

MOSES,
THE YOUTH PASTOR

Finding a perfect "youth pastor" role model in the Bible has been one of my goals during seminary life. There are many great biblical role models for preachers, missionaries, and church leaders, but not youth pastors! Of course, the perfect "model" for any ministry is always Jesus. He is, however, beyond my ability to imitate due to his perfectly human and perfectly divine natures. Paul and Peter, who preach powerful sermons and reveal many miraculous signs in various mission fields, can be "the next top model" for youth pastors based on their passion for Christ, but they do not sign up for the youth pastor position in their context. In fact, the Bible does not offer a clear role model of youth pastors since the concepts of adolescence and youth ministry are relatively new ones.

In Deuteronomy, however, I found a significant correlation between the teachings of Moses and the contemporary needs of youth ministry. The great prophet Moses represents "an old generation in the process of dying [that] teaches faith to another generation maturing into life."[19] This concept of passing on faith from an old generation to the next generation is also the essence of contemporary youth ministry. For the growing adolescents, the role of youth ministry is to provide a space, both physical and spiritual, for the nurturing of the organic faith so they may continue to live as healthy people of God. At the end of his life, Moses has a similar concern for his youth members. He is desperate to pass on the organic faith that he has throughout his life to the next generation who are about to enter the Promised Land. Moses, therefore, is a helpful youth pastor role model for those who have similar concerns of passing on the faith to the younger generation of today. Considering Moses as the youth pastor for his community, and borrowing Dennis Olson's idea of the five modes of Deuteronomic catechesis, I will propose that the youth ministry of today must be theologically centered, humanly adaptable, form-critically inclusive, socially transformative, and communally-oriented.[20] Moreover, I will explain why these ancient catechesis of Moses and the characteristics of Moses himself still offer the essential principles of the organic faith to the 21st century youth pastors.

The Five Youth Ministry Principles of Moses

The goal of catechesis is clear throughout human history: to educate the next generation about the faith. For both Judaism and Christianity, therefore, catechesis has been the way to pass on their faith throughout the generations. Catechesis in Deuteronomy, however, seems to play more than an educating or socializing role to a new generation in the community's tradition. It goes beyond interest in teaching basic "Christianity 101" to the younger generation for its own spiritual well-being. Catechesis in the book

---

[19] Dennis T. Olson, *Deuteronomy and the Death of Moses*, 21.
[20] In his book, *Deuteronomy and the Death of Moses*, Dennis Olson offers five helpful corollaries of Deuteronomy catechesis. He states that the catechesis in Deuteronomy is theologically centered, humanly adaptable, form-critically inclusive, socially transformative, and communally oriented one. I will use these five corollaries as the basic cardinal principles of Moses' teaching ministry to his youth members (Olson, 11).

of Deuteronomy includes elements of covenant, sermon, law code, and constitution for the community of faith. In other words, Deuteronomy includes instructions of

> structured relationship, proclamation, the role of law, summation of the community identity and practice, as well as ... the role of teaching, passing the faith from one generation to the next, the focus on the family as well as the larger national community, the focus on theology and its practical implications for daily life. [21]

These elements in Moses' catechism are what contemporary youth ministry needs to reclaim. Olson's five corollaries based on the above richness of Moses' catechesis offer five essential ministry principles for youth ministry. Similar to the catechesis of Moses, contemporary youth ministry that promotes organic faith must be theologically centered, humanly adaptable, form-critically inclusive, socially transformative, and communally-oriented in order to effectively pass on the faith to the next generation.

Youth Ministry as a Theologically-Centered Ministry

If Moses can be portrayed as the youth pastor of his time, his youth ministry is a theologically-centered one. Moses' teaching in Deuteronomy is primarily about God and the Word of God. It is a theological education that springs from the Word of God to establish the right relationship between God and humanity, between humans, and between humanity and the wider world of nature. For this reason, Walter Brueggemann calls Deuteronomy "the theological center of the Old Testament," [22] or for Olson, "the closest thing we have in the Old Testament to a systematic

---

[21] Ibid., 10.
[22] Walter Brueggemann, *The Creative Word: Canon as a Model for Biblical Education*, 37.

catechism or theology."[23] Moreover, as Fretheim asserts, "a theological agenda pervades the entire book [of Deuteronomy], but it is an applied theology, concerned to move the hearts and minds of the audience. At heart, the book focuses on the proper relationship between Israel and its God, essential if Israel is to have a future."[24] Not only is Moses the great leader and law giver who leads the Israelites out of slavery in Egypt, but he is also the most influential practical theologian in his "youth ministry" who leads the next generation in having a right relationship with God.

Moses knows that his job as a youth pastor is to teach the community about who the LORD is through the retelling of what the LORD has done for Israel. Remembering what the LORD has done for Israel forms the crucial theological foundation in Moses' youth ministry. The history of the Israelites (Deut. 1-4), the Ten Commandments (Deut. 5), and other "remembering and don't forget" preaching (Deut. 6:20-25, 8) constantly remind the Israelites that "the LORD God is one LORD" (Deut. 6:4) who brought them out of Egypt with a mighty hand and led them to the land that God promised by oath to their forefathers.

Remembering what the LORD has done in and through the history of humanity, therefore, must be the theological starting point of youth ministry. The best way to teach youth about *who* the LORD is, by retelling what the LORD has done for God's people throughout human history. This teaching should not be solely limited to remembering of the God of Israel (Old Testament) and the God of the Cross (New Testament). It also needs to include the stories of God's actions for each contemporary youth member or each community, as they must also remember their own unique experience with God. For example, for Korean-American youth, they need to remember what God has done for their parents or the people of Korea because it offers valuable insight of cultural hermeneutics into the heritage of their faith. It offers intergenerational faith dialogue about the faithfulness of the same God. Moreover, knowing that each culture or context has its

---

[23] Olson, 11.
[24] Terrance E. Fretheim, *The Pentateuch*, 154.

unique experience of God helps youth to understand that God reveals God's divine self in various ways.

Both Moses and Jesus teach their students to love the LORD with all their heart, soul, and strength (Deut. 6:5, Matt. 22:37). This command is meaningless to the youth members unless the LORD is a personal God to them. For the Israelites, the LORD is their God who brought them out of Egypt to the Promised Land. For Jesus, the LORD is the *abba* Father who sent him, the only Son, to the world of humanity to show God's love and grace for all. From this unique relationship with God, both Moses and Jesus can command their audience to wholeheartedly love the LORD. Youth members of today also need the personal reason to love the LORD their God. Since we all have different experiences of God, and God works in different ways, every individual's faith is a unique faith and each one's love of God is wholeheartedly personal as well. The theologically-centered youth ministry teaches about God of Abraham, Isaac, Jacob, Moses, the Israelites, the Early Church, as well as contemporary youth members and their family.

Youth Ministry as a Humanly-Adaptable Ministry.

At the end of his life, Moses is instructing the generation who has not experienced God in the same way as the older generation. One of the goals of Moses' youth ministry is, therefore, not to offer the final and exhaustive theology of God to the next generation based only on one's experience, but to teach the faithfulness of God is a humanly-adaptable one in various contexts. Olson suggests that "the image of an ongoing journey is central to Deuteronomy's vision of catechesis."[25] The ministry that Moses has in his mind, therefore, is a humanly adaptable one as one faces different contexts. Moses himself suggests that God will provide a new prophet after him to further instruct the people of God in the Promised Land (Deut. 18:15). Deuteronomy chapters 29-32 further establish "mechanisms for ongoing human teaching and

---

[25] Olson, 12.

interpretation in future generations."[26] There is no doubt that contemporary youth ministry must have the same attitude of treating the ministry of youth as an ongoing and adaptive teaching process.

Youth ministers need to have flexible and adaptable minds in the post-modern world context, but they must be careful not to eliminate the Word of God for a new generation for the sake of "adaptability." The book of Deuteronomy conveys the process of exposition and exploration of the Torah for the new generation, but this ongoing journey is firmly centered on the Word of God. Moses and other leaders of Israel's way of teaching might be different, but the core of their teaching, the Word of God, is the same. Youth ministry must not forget that the role of bringing in different kinds of music, arts, programs, and activities is to adapt to the current culture for the sake of teaching the Word of God to teenagers. Music and other activities can be used as a part of the proclamation of the Word, but it must not replace the Word of God for the sake of cultural adaptability. Humanly adaptable youth ministry continues to seek the Word of God as the heart of its ever-changing process for the new generation.

If the theologically-centered youth ministry convinces youth that God is faithful throughout the generations, the humanly-adaptable youth ministry teaches that God's faithfulness has been revealed through various human conditions in the history of humanity. Even God's plan through Jesus Christ was a humanly-adaptable one: the WORD became flesh so God can dwell among humanity. By being sensitive to various contexts and cultures, and be humanly-adaptable to different methods, God's faithfulness can be further proclaimed and confirmed.

Youth Ministry as a Generation-Inclusive Ministry

The book of Deuteronomy takes its audience directly to the heart of Israel's faith with a variety of methods and forms. The first

---

[26] Ibid., 12.

youth pastor, Moses, conveys a greater concern for the transmission of the faith to the next generation with various forms in one book. Deuteronomy includes law codes, covenants, and constitutions to reach its goal. Olson explains the advantage of this form-critically inclusive catechesis in Moses' youth ministry:

> The use of catechesis as a genre designation for Deuteronomy takes advantage of its capacity to include a variety of other subforms or genres found in individual sections of Deuteronomy. The form of Deuteronomy as a whole includes elements of a law code, a covenant, and a constitution. The term catechesis or catechism is able to incorporate elements of these prior forms under its umbrella, elements that are clearly present in the final form of Deuteronomy: words/narratives, commandments, statutes and ordinances, speeches, covenant, song, blessing, and so on. Deuteronomic catechesis uses a variety of methods and forms to achieve its goal.[27]

In order to achieve the goal of transferring organic faith, Deuteronomy uses a variety of methods and forms. For the youth ministry of today, this form-critically inclusive lesson can be translated as a *generation-inclusive* approach.

If the humanly-adaptable ministry teaches us to adapt various cultural and contextual factors of contemporary youth life into youth ministry, the ministry-critical inclusive teaching challenges youth pastors to broaden the boundary of youth ministry by including various ministries. The form of youth ministry as a whole must include a variety of youth-related ministries, such as family ministry, academic and school ministry, interpersonal and intrapersonal relationship related ministry, and contemplative ministry. The term "youth ministry" must move beyond the boundary of the Sunday worship for youth, the Saturday night youth Bible study, or the praise and prayer nights. For example,

---

[27] Olson, 12.

family ministry dealing with educating the parents regarding contemporary teenagers' life cannot be excluded from youth ministry curriculum. The church needs to be concerned about the youth's family lives and know their parents, since it is the parents who hold the most influential key of educating their children.

The importance of the parents' teaching role is very clear in Moses' youth ministry as well. Moses instructs the parents to "impress, talk, tie, and write" the commandments to their children in order to reinforce the commandment (Deut. 6:6-9). Moses further instructs parents to teach their children about God and God's actions with the Israelites. Proverbs also emphasizes the essential role of parents in youth ministry. After the lesson of "the fear of the LORD is the beginning of knowledge" (Prov. 1:7), the writer of the Proverbs urges youth to listen to their parents.[28] Both parents are obligated instruct their children to "fear the LORD." Perhaps the reason why there is no specific youth ministry guide in the Scriptures is because it was an assumed education and ministry for all parents.

Not only were the ancient parents expected to be the youth pastors and teachers for their children, but the parents of the Reformation era as well. In his sermon *The Estate of Marriage*, Martin Luther asserts the crucial role of father and mother as a spiritual teacher to their children,

> Most certainly father and mother are apostles, bishops, and priests to their children, for it is they who make them acquainted with the Gospel. In short there is no greater or nobler authority on earth than that of parents over their children, for this authority is both spiritual and temporal.[29]

---

[28] "Listen, my son, to your father's instruction and do not forsake your mother's teaching" (Prov. 1:8).
[29] Quoted by Strommen and Hardel, *Passing on the Faith: A radical New Model for Youth and Family Ministry*, p. 28). Strommen and Hardel's book offers an excellent youth ministry model that places family as the heart of the ministry.

It seems that the modern and post-modern concept of "adolescence" that forced many parents to seek "professional" adolescent educators, including youth pastors. Youth ministry cannot be separated from family ministry which reinforces the spiritual teaching role of parents.

One's job as a youth minister is not only to build relationships with and serve teenagers an weekends, but also to include all varieties of ministries in which our youth are involved. This does not mean that one needs to become the ultimate problem solver for the youth. However, youth ministers need to become the ultimate problem *recognizer* in every possible aspect of a youth's life. It requires more work and effort for youth pastors, but that is a part of the calling. We are spiritual leaders and pastors for youth, but at the same time, we are also family counselors, parent educators, academic advisors, and pastoral caregivers. Youth ministry, therefore, must have the mindset of the *generation-inclusive* approach.

Youth Ministry as a Socially-Transformative Ministry

Right before the grand entrance into the Promised Land, Moses initiates one of the most powerful youth revivals. By hearing the LORD's words and remembering the things that the LORD has done for them, the next generation are encouraged by Moses to socially transform their lives so they may not "turn aside to the right or to the left and walk in all the way that the LORD God has commanded [them]" (Deut. 5:32-33). This demand of transformation of their hearts and attitudes before entering the Promised Land is critical because Moses, from his experience, knows how wicked and rebellious this new generation can become. The desert for Moses is the place where he experiences God's providence and mercy. At the same time, the desert represents the painful place where the unfaithful generation, including Moses, fails to fully obey and trust God. On the border of the Promised Land, Moses demands the total transformation of his youth members. Through the circumcision of their heart, they must set their mind on God so they may "love [God] with all [their] heart and with all [their soul], and live" (Deut. 30:6).

This transformative teaching of Moses challenges today's youth pastors to reclaim the same power that shapes and transforms the thoughts, attitudes, and behaviors of adolescents and whole communities.[30] Similar to Moses' context, youth ministry of today is in a transitioning period that demands the social transformation of the youth's hearts for the Kingdom of God. Youth are at the bank of their own "Jordan River" to enter the Promised Land called the "adult world." Many of our youth are eager to enter the "adult world," because the land of the adulthood often has been falsely portrayed as the place of freedom from the parents. Similar to Moses' new generation, our youths are eager to enter the land of freedom and prosperity. In the Promised Land, however, awaits many "other gods" who will tempt the new generation away from wholly loving the LORD.

Olson's investigation on these "other gods" in Deuteronomy offers vital lesson to today's youth. By observing Deuteronomy 7-10 with less culture-specific eyes, Olson argues that "other gods" in Deuteronomy reflect not only upon other gods of ancient Israelite religion (El, Baal, Asherah, etc.), but "three other gods or idols who were more insidious and more universal threats to the singular commitment to Yahweh."[31] "The triad of three temptations," as Olson labels, is militarism (political or natural powers), self sufficient materialism, and self-righteousness moralism.[32] These "other gods" also appear together in the same text in Isaiah 47, Ecclesiastes 2-3, and the Psalms 10.[33] Along with these scriptures, Deuteronomy challenges the contemporary youth pastors to reaffirm the first commandment to the youth members, "you shall have no other gods before me."

The youth in today's world faces the exact same temptation of serving "other gods." The war against terrorist and the U.S.

---

[30] Olson, 13.
[31] Olson, 52.
[32] Ibid. 53.
[33] For the further explanation, please read "Deuteronomy 7-10: The Gods of Death-Militarism, Materialism, and Moralism section" (p. 52-58) in Olson's book.

military power continues to mistakenly teach the teenagers about achieving "justice" through human ability and calculation. The glorious war movies and T.V. dramas further venerate the power of militarism to the youth, especially to American teenagers. I can recall my high school teaching moment when I sensed the clear presence of the militarism among American teenagers. When I tried to convince my students to study harder because the American students' performance on mathematics was ranked lower than other nations, one of my students proudly responded back to me by saying, "that's OK because we have the best army in the world anyway." Violence and war must not be the expression of power to adolescents of today, at least among the youth ministry members.

The self-sufficient materialism and self-righteousness moralism are the two other "gods" that continue to threaten teenagers having the right relationship with God. Against the message of all-powerful materialism in our society, Moses and Jesus' message is clear, "one does not live by bread alone, but by every word that comes from the mouth of the LORD" (Duet. 8:3). Similarly, both Moses and Jesus also confirm their position on the self-righteousness moralism. Moses speaks to the Israelites, "do not say in your heart, 'It is because of my righteousness that the Lord has brought me to occupy this land'" (Deut. 9:4); Jesus confirms the same message through the parable of the Pharisee and the tax collector, "for everyone who exalts himself will be humbled, and he who humbles himself will be exalted" (Luke 18:14). The church of Jesus Christ must not promote the "Moralistic Therapeutic Deism" that teaches the youth to become "good, nice, and fair" people so that they may feel happy about themselves. The youth ministry must speak against self-sufficient materialism and self-righteous moralism by nurturing the youth with the Word of God so that they can socially transform their lives to be the witnesses of the Cross.

The socially-transformative youth ministry, therefore, teaches teenagers to seek God's justice in their school classrooms, neighborhood streets, shopping malls, and church communities. It further cultivates socially-transformed youth members who firmly reject to make their allegiance to militarism, materialism, and moralism.

Youth Ministry as a Communally-Oriented Ministry

The last ministry principle from Moses is the most obvious yet challenging one: cultivating a communally-oriented ministry. The emphasis on communal life is obvious since Christian life by definition means a communal life as one body of Christ. On the other hand, it is challenging because of inadequate theological notions of the communal life among the youth. Youth members often hear about the typical Christian teaching of the importance of community and communal life. Their conception of the faith community, however, quite often does not include the wide variety of relationships. For example, not many teenagers consider the life of faith as a communal enterprise outside of their church youth group. As a result, they consider the church ground as the only communal place of faith and their youth group members as the only proper spiritual partners. In order to build a genuine "communally-oriented" youth ministry, we must introduce the importance of including various types of communal relationships in the broad circle of "faith community," which includes the past and the future generations of believers.

A typical communal life model in youth ministry can be described as a two dimensional relationship triangle. God is on top, the self is on the one corner, and the other youth members are on the other corner.

Diagram A

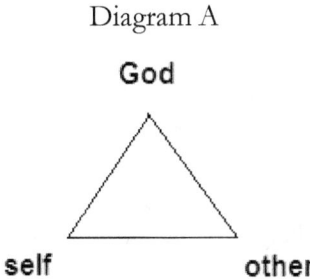

For many youth members, this diagram represents their communal life in a youth group. God is at top or center of their community (hopefully), and through this connection to the same God, a youth member (self) and the other members are connected to each other. This is not necessarily a wrong view of a faith community because it offers significant theological truth about our faith community. God is at the top or center of any Christian communal life and relationship, and we are connected not only to God but to one another through the same God. This triangular relationship diagram, however, offers a limited view of communally-oriented youth ministry. The main problem of this diagram is the inability to perceive other communal lives that a youth member is already engaging both in and outside their youth group community.[34]

Moses' understanding of a communally-oriented youth ministry goes beyond the two-dimensional triangular form. At the end of his life, Moses knows that he will not be with this new generation physically. The physical absence of Moses, however, does not imply the exclusion of Moses from the communal life of the new generation. Moses is a part of a faith community in the future generations because Moses belongs to the God of all generations. In this sense, not only Moses, but the past generation of who served the same God shares the communal life of the present and the future generations. Olson further explains:

> "Deuteronomy deals with the wide variety of relationships – God's relationship to humans, human relationships within the faith community, the relationship of the people of God to other peoples, and nations, and the relationship of humans to creation. The various functions of community are treated: worshiping, witnessing, marrying, parenting, governing, adjudicating, loving, rejoicing, learning, farming, buying, selling, cooking, and working. Deuteronomy even creates

---

[34] Even the relationship among the youth group members can be problematic. They may be a communally-oriented group at the youth group meetings or at the youth retreat camps, but when they go back to their home or school, they are no longer sharing this communal life. Absence of physical presence in a youth group often breaks even the notion of this two dimensional communal life in a youth group.

communities across generational lines: the present-day community becomes one with generations past and generations future (4:25-31; 5"3-5; 28:36-46).[35]

Moses' concern of a communal life in God includes the past and the future generations because the God cannot be understood apart from the past and the future generations of faith. God to Moses and the rest of Israelites at the river of Jordan is the God of the past generation who made a covenant with them, and the God of the future generation who is about to fulfill the promise. Although Moses knows he will not see the fulfillment of God's promise, in the God of the past and the future, he is a communal member of the future generation of the Promised Land.

The boundary of the life of faith as a communal activity in a youth group, therefore, needs to be broadened. Instead of a two-dimensional triangular relationship, a three-dimensional cone-shaped relationship describes the meaning of communal life more accurately.

<u>Diagram B[36]</u>

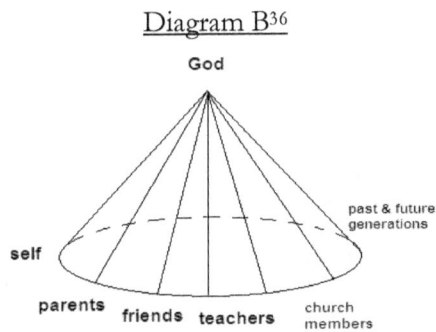

A youth member in this communally-oriented ministry is intimately tied to God and is interdependent and responsive in his

---

[35] Olson, 13.
[36] Kenda Dean offers similar diagram to explain a three-dimensional view of intimacy. Through the "Three-Dimensional Structure of Faith," Dean argues that "authentic intimacy requires the presence of a transcendent Other who sheds light on us from beyond ourselves" (Dean, *Practicing Passion*, 130-101).

or her relationship to others, including family members, friends, teachers, church adult members, and the past and future generations at the same time. In other words, since all humanity is related to the LORD who is beyond times and places, a youth member is sharing the communal life of faith with anyone around him or her in the present moment as well as the past and the future times. This is only possible because every communal life throughout the human history is connected to the same God. The faith community, the church of Jesus Christ, does not belong to one youth group, but the whole body of Christ. A youth member in this church of Christ must then remember that he or she is a part of much bigger communal life in God.[37]

This cone-shaped perspective of the communal life of faith further makes a youth member a genuinely "responsible" person as a disciple of Christ in the present time. H. R. Niebuhr's concept of "the Responsible Self" offers helpful insight. In his book, Niebuhr considers every human being a responding agent. Humans are always responding to some kinds of influence, such as God, other human beings, a community, the natural order or history, or their self. Since God is in control of all human affairs, the "fitting response" of Christians to other human beings must reflect the

---

[37] Jurgen Moltmann further offers theological reasoning of including the past generation into the current community of faith: "The community of Christ is a community not only of the living but of the dead as well. It is not just a community of 'brothers and sisters'; it is a community of mothers and daughters, and of fathers and sons – or of mothers and sons, and fathers and daughters. In Rom. 14.9 Paul writes: 'For to this end Christ died and lived again, that he might be Lord both of the dead and of the living.' His sovereignty over the dead is not yet the resurrection of the dead but is only as yet their saving reception into the community of Christ. When he 'descended into hell' (the realm of the dead), as the Creed puts it, Christ broke the power of death and took the dead into his fellowship. So the community of Christ is in him a community of the living with the dead, and of the dead with the living. In the risen Christ, the wall of death has been broken down. So in this community with Christ the dead are not 'dead' in the modern sense; they 'have a presence'" (Jurgen Moltmann, *In the End-The Beginning: The life of hope*, 135). This broaden concept of the community of Christ can help youth members to place themselves in a greater community of faith than just their youth group. By including themselves in the past clouds of faithful witnesses of Christ, youth members will gain better idea of who they are in the line of God's history.

characteristics of God. The cone-shaped communal life of a youth member requires similar "fitting responses." Since God is God of righteousness, love, mercy, grace, etc. to all humanity, youth members need to "respond" or reflect such characteristics of God as children of God.

Moreover, youth members are responsible to God's actions in the past, present, and the future because the youth members have a relationship with this God who transcends time and place. Through this relationship with God, youth members are now responsible for continuing a life of faith that the past faithful generations have established. At the same time, they are responsible to pass on this faith that reflects God's faithfulness, love, mercy, and grace to the future generation. In other words, youth pastors are passing the faith to youth members so they can do the same thing for the next generation. In this concept of community of faith, our youth members will live their lives responsibly to the clouds of witnesses that have come before and will come soon.

The Death of Moses, the End of our Youth Ministry.

The death of Moses in the book of Deuteronomy challenges contemporary youth pastors regarding their attitudes about youth ministry. Moses is determined to educate the next generation because his "end" means the "beginning" of the next generation. His death foreshadows the birth of the new people of God. It is a life and death issue for both Moses and his youth members. Not only is the content of this education--loving God wholeheartedly-- a life and death matter, but teaching and mediating the holy Word of God is a life-threatening job: "for who is there of all flesh that has heard the voice of the living God... and remained alive?" (Deut. 5:26). By taking the office of mediator, by facing God's holiness for the future generation, Moses had to face his "premature death."[38] As mediators of God's holy Word to the

---

[38] Olson, 47.

younger generation, youth pastors may also have to face the "premature death."

Moses' "premature death" outside of the Promised Land teaches three crucial lessons to youth ministers. First, it means the death of one's own ambition. Moses, the greatest prophet Israel ever had (Deut. 34:10-12), decided to let his own ambitions die by refusing to accept God's offer of establishing a whole new nation through Moses' name (Deut. 9:14). When Moses had a chance to make his name even greater than Abraham or Jacob, he decided to let go of his ambition for the sake of the "stiff necked" people. Moreover, Moses' death outside the Land conveyed the message that his own ambition alone cannot lead the Israelites into the Promised Land. In the end, it is God who enters the Land with the new generation. It is God who produces the healthy fruits.

The youth pastors who wish to cultivate the organic faith must let their own ambition die as well. The ambition of gaining fame as a successful youth pastor or the ambition to lead every youth member to the "Promised Land" with one's own systematic youth program must die before God. Similar to Moses, youth pastors may not enter the Promised Land with their youth members. Similar to Moses, youth pastors' role may be to struggle and wander with the youth members in the desert of the postmodern world. Whether the youth members enter this Promised Land belongs to God and God alone. Borrowing from Mother Teresa's teaching, God has not called youth pastors to be successful or ambitious workers, but to be faithful servants of God. Our joy of being youth ministers must be founded in the goodness of God, not our own ambition or the results of such an ambition.

Secondly, "the premature death" conveys the urgency of teaching the absolute necessity of the LORD God in youth members' life. Unlike Moses, youth pastors rarely have to physically die by taking the office of mediator in these days. The attitudes of youth pastors, however, must be the same as Moses as who urgently delivered the message of God as the mediator and interpreter of God's Word until his death. Youth pastors need to approach ministries radically and urgently like Moses, since mediating the Word of God is a fundamentally dangerous and urgent job. The question of "how will God's word be mediated to the people and to succeeding generations so that the relationship of God and [the future generation] may be continued?"[39] presupposes the death of the old and the birth of the new generation. Youth pastors are the dying generation who are "responsible" to mediate the Word of God to the next generation. Youth pastors must not delay this responsibility of educating the youth for any reason. It is a serious and urgent matter.

The second chapter of the book of Judges conveys a similar message. The generation after Joshua failed to wholeheartedly serve the LORD God. Joshua's generation, who were the students of Moses, failed to pass on the faith that they had received from God through Moses. What happened to Joshua's generation who received an excellent catechism from Moses? One noticeable answer can be the different leadership style between Moses and Joshua. Both Moses and Joshua were great leaders for the people, but only Moses played a role of youth pastor by risking his life as a mediator of the Word of God to the younger generation with an urgent heart.[40] Joshua obeyed and followed God's instruction faithfully but the urgency of educating the community about the *absolute necessity* of the LORD God in their lives seems lacking in his ministry. Similar to Moses, Joshua offers a choice to serve the LORD: "if serving the LORD seems undesirable to you, then choose for yourselves this day whom you will serve" (Josh. 24:15a). This also echoes Elijah's speech at the battles story against the Baal prophets: "If the LORD is God, follow him; but if Baal is God,

---

[39] Olson, 47.
[40] It is not fair to "blame" Joshua for the Israel's rebellion against the LORD. Certainly, it is not his fault. Moses himself also "failed" leading his own generation to be a faithful generation. But because of that failed experience, Moses had this urgency in his teaching to his youth members. The difference that I am emphasizing here is this urgent heart of Moses, which Joshua seemed lacking. Whether one generation becomes God's faithful generation or not solely depends on God's grace. My argument is that giving choices of trusting God to the youth members is not sufficient enough. Youth pastors must command to choose God so that youth and their family may live. Although we must acknowledge that we do not have all the answers regarding God and God's work upon humanity, especially in the post-modern land of relativism, we do have to express at least one definite conviction of our faith: "Jesus is the way, truth, and life, so choose him."

follow him" (1 Kings 18:21). In contrast to Joshua and Elijah, Moses commands what to choose in his preaching,

> This day I call heaven and earth as witnesses against you that I have set before you life and death, blessings and curses. Now choose life, so that you and your children may live and that you may love the LORD your God, listen to his voice, and hold fast to him. For the LORD is your life, and he will give you many years in the land he swore to give to your fathers, Abraham, Isaac and Jacob (Deut. 30:19-20).

Both Joshua's and Elijah's preaching do not convey such a firm and urgent message of the absolute necessity of the LORD God to the entire community. At the end of his sermon, Joshua proclaims, "but as for me and my household, we will serve the LORD" (Josh. 24:15b). The result of his preaching suggests that the audience of Joshua reaffirms their dedication to the LORD. Unfortunately, the rest of the generation after Joshua seems to lose their faith again.

Youth pastors need to exceed Joshua's "as for me and my household" ministry mentality in a contemporary context. Moses' concern for serving the LORD goes beyond the boundary of "me and my household." Moses' youth ministry concerns all members of community about the absolute truth of living in the presence of God. The stories throughout the Bible evidently suggest that it is not a matter of choice. Fearing the LORD and serving him with all faithfulness is not an option for our youth members. Especially in today's pluralistic and advertisement-saturated society where all too many choices are given to teenagers, God cannot be an option for them. Following Christ with their own cross is the only way to find their true identity in this world. The post-modernist says, "I don't know about you but as for me and my household we will serve the LORD." Christ did not only die for "me and my household," but for all humanity. As mediators of this good news to youth, and like Paul and Silas, preaching the Word of God for both "me and my household" and "you and your household" (Acts 16:31) are indispensable.

Finally, the death of Moses conveys God's blessing, promise, and hope through "the priority of divine over human action."[41] At the end of his fabulous career and at the climax of his youth ministry right before the grand entrance to the Promised Land, Moses faces death before God at Mount Nebo. At the end of his ministry, Moses dies, and God takes over. Olson writes:

> After Moses 'went up' to Mount Nebo, Yahweh takes over the action of the verbs – showing, speaking, commanding, and burying. The only action that Moses does is 'die.' This section of chapter 34 is in tune with the emphasis of the Moab covenant in chapters 29-32, stressing the priority of divine over human action.[42]

No matter how good the youth program is or how successful youth pastor one may become, it is God who has the final word on our youth ministry. Thus, accepting the irrefutable human limitation before God is part of youth pastors' condition. It is specifically this condition that allows youth workers to receive the irresistible blessing, promise, and hope of God Although God did not allow Moses to enter the Promised Land with his youth members, God *showed* him the whole land (Deut. 34:1). Before Moses' death, in the end of his youth ministry career, Moses witnesses God's blessing, promise, and hope for the new generation.

This is the most hopeful eschatological truth; at the end, there is God who is compassionate and gracious, slow to anger, abounding in love and faithfulness (Ex. 34:6). The end of any youth ministry, there is the same God. Moses' premature death teaches and reminds youth pastors that youth ministry is beyond their control, thus they must solely trust God and place divine action prior to theirs. As much as youth pastors teach the youth members

---

[41] Olson, 167.
[42] Ibid., 167.

to trust in the LORD with all their heart (Prov. 3:5), youth pastors need to fully trust the triune God as well about the outcome of their ministries. Youth pastors must remember that it is the LORD who blesses and keeps youth, who makes God's divine face shine upon them and be gracious to them, and who turns God's divine face toward the youth and give them peace (Num. 6:23-26).

Summary of Moses' Cultivating Manual

Without a mediator, there is no passing on faith. Both Moses and Jesus proved such a crucial point. But their "premature death" once again teaches a critical lesson for youth pastors about being a mediator. It is a dangerous job because youth pastors are dealing with the Word of God that is "living and active, sharper than any double-edged sword" (Heb. 4:12 a). This Word of God "penetrates even to dividing soul and spirit, joints and marrow; it judges the thoughts and attitudes of the heart" (Heb. 4:12 b). God's Word gives life and hope for all who seek God, but it is extremely dangerous.

Moses is the living example of Deuteronomy who showed how to live with this "dangerously good" Word of God as a human being and how to cultivate organic faith to the next generation as a youth pastor. By framing his ministry as theologically-centered, humanly-adaptable, ministry-critical inclusive, socially-transformative, and communally-oriented one, Moses faithfully delivered the absolute necessity of the LORD God to his youth members. "The premature death" of Moses is the burden that youth pastors need to carry on throughout their career. This "premature death," however, means "hopeful birth" for the new generation because God's blessing, promise, and hope is with this generation. Although youth pastors may not enter the Promised Land with the new generation, youth pastors should not be disappointed. Nonetheless, youth pastors are a part of the clouds of faithful gardeners, whom God has called to cultivate and mediate of the "dangerously good" Word of God to the "dangerously good" groups of adolescents.

CHAPTER FOUR

THE STAYING POWER OF JEONG (정)

Brian White was the first non-Korean youth pastor for Praise Church while I was serving the same church as a director of Christian education. He carried out his ministry very well, and the youth members had a meaningful time with him. Although he only served for a year, the disappointment of many youth members was enormous when they heard that Brian was leaving for Japan as a missionary. The youth group gave a memorable farewell to Brian as he left for the mission field. About a month later, three Jr. High members came and asked me whether they could organize a talent show to raise mission funds for Brian. These teenagers, who had no previous experience of fund raising for mission work, came together as a small group to express their willingness to help their former youth pastor. They had no clue how to organize their fund raising event, but I could tell from their eyes that they were sincere about their proposal. As an education pastor for children and youth, I was thrilled to hear their voluntary proposal. Even more exciting, however, was seeing their genuine affection and longing for their former pastor who stayed with them for only a short period of time. Brian was not only a good youth pastor for them, but a youth pastor with whom they shared the love, affection, attachment, compassion, and heart of Christ.

From Brian's farewell speech, his own affectionate feelings had been expressed as "good and memorable moments" that he will never forget. From my Korean-American cultural hermeneutical perspective, however, the affectionate feeling that both Brian and his youth members shared is what the Korean tradition calls *jeong* ("love"[43]). It is this concept of *jeong* that I recognize from the youth members' heart when they came together for the fundraising idea. Although they may not have recognized this Korean word, the expression of the Korean/Asian concept of *jeong* was clearly present in their hearts, and it came out powerfully in this youth ministry context.[44] If youth pastors in the KA context can understand the significance of *jeong* in this culture, practice it properly with KA teenagers, and theologically frame it into youth ministry, then *jeong* can become one the most powerful cultivating tools in the KA church context.

The Meaning of Jeong

The Korean concept of *jeong* has a multidimensional meaning which cannot be fully translated in English. "Love" is the simplest translation; however most Koreans would not be fully

---

[43] If I have to pick one word translation for *jeong*, it would be "love" or "attachment." I will define the term *jeong* in greater depth later.
[44] I do not believe the concept of *jeong* is a uniquely Korean or Asian "thing" that no other ethnic group can experience. I have experienced this *jeong* from various ethnic groups throughout my life. My argument is not to prove this concept of uniquely Korean/Asian, but to argue that the recognition and the role of *jeong* among Korean descendents are uniquely different from other ethnic groups. *Jeong* is deeply rooted in Korean culture, and Korean people have been uniquely conceptualized and shared it unlike any other ethnic groups.

satisfied with this translation due to the complexity of the concept of *jeong*. One Korean-English dictionary defines *jeong* as "feeling, love, affection, attachment, sentiment, passion, human nature, sympathy, empathy, heart, and compassion." Even all of these English words combined cannot delineate a complete meaning of *jeong*. It includes all of this, and more. One simply cannot concisely define *jeong* without losing the insightful of its multiple dimensions. Furthermore, the word is used with many other Korean words to make different words. For example, *Mo-jeong*, in a simplest level, means maternal affection, while *Woo-jeong* represents a friendship. Or while *Yul-jeong* means a passion, *Dong-jeong* denotes compassion. Due to various derived forms of the word *jeong*, it would be impossible to fully describe the meaning of it to those who have not experienced *jeong* within this cultural context.

For the purpose of youth pastors in KA context my definition of *jeong* will be strictly limited within a theological framework in the context of youth ministry. I will explore three different types of *jeong* (*woo-jeong, ae-jeong, mo-jeong*)[45] to propose a *jeong*-based youth ministry in Korean American context. The concept of *woo-jeong* focuses on the relationship between two friends; thus it is a bi-relational concept. Through *woo-jeong*, youth members can build a stronger bond of loyalty between one another in the community of Christ. Youth pastors can also establish this *woo-jeong* with their youth members to build stronger relationships. *Woo-jeong* offers "staying power" between individuals.

While *woo-jeong* requires mutual relationship, *ae-jeong* does not. If *woo-jeong* is considered as shared *jeong* between two friends, *ae-jeong* is more a one-way personal affection towards something(s). It is often considered that *ae-jeong* is stronger than *woo-jeong* in Korean culture because it is more personal than *woo-jeong*. I will propose that this *ae-jeong* is what youth ministers also need to acquire in addition to *woo-jeong* to be a *jeong*-based youth pastor. A youth pastor in Korean American church context needs to build *ae-*

---

[45] *Woo-jeong* means friendship; *ae-jeong* means loving affection towards an object or a person; and *mo-jeong* literally means "maternal" love, but I will use the term for "parental" love instead to include both father and mother's love.

jeong towards one's own youth ministry. Youth pastors' own *ae-jeong* towards their ministries will provide another "staying power" that supports youth pastors to stay *in* the ministry and be faithful to the calling in times of trouble.

Finally, the concept of *mo-jeong* will explicate another "staying power" -- staying in relationship with God. The word *mo-jeong* denotes unconditional love that can only be experienced from parents. While the meaning of *woo-jeong* and *ae-jeong* will be used as a relationship guideline between two individuals or a youth pastor to a youth ministry, the concept of *mo-jeong* will serve as a framework of expressing the loving relationship between God to an individual. Similar to *ae-jeong*, it can be portrayed as one-way expression of love. Unlike *woo-jeong* and *ae-jeong*, however, we have no control over *mo-jeong*. It belongs to God and God alone. We are the beneficiary of God's *mo-jeong*. By exploring the concept of *mo-jeong* through the God of Israel and the God of the Cross, I will explain how God offers God's "staying power" to sustain God's relationship with God's people. It is in this *mo-jeong* (God's love) that any other type of *jeong* can find its true meaning.

The essence of *jeong* is the concept of "sticky staying power" in three dimensional relationships in a youth group. The goal of the *jeong*-based youth ministry is, therefore, to employ this "staying power" between youth members and youth members, youth pastors and their ministries (or "callings"), and God and youth members (and youth pastors) to holistically transform our youth and youth pastors to be Kingdom workers of Christ.[46]

---

[46] I agree with Dean and Foster regarding the term "relational ministry." I also prefer the term *incarnational* to *relational* when I speak of ministry. But I will not discuss the difference in this paper due to the scope of the paper (see page 26-28 of *The God Bearing Life* for further discussion). For the simplicity of my paper, I will use "relational" rather than "incarnational" to develop my argument.

The Framework of Youth Ministry of *Jeong*

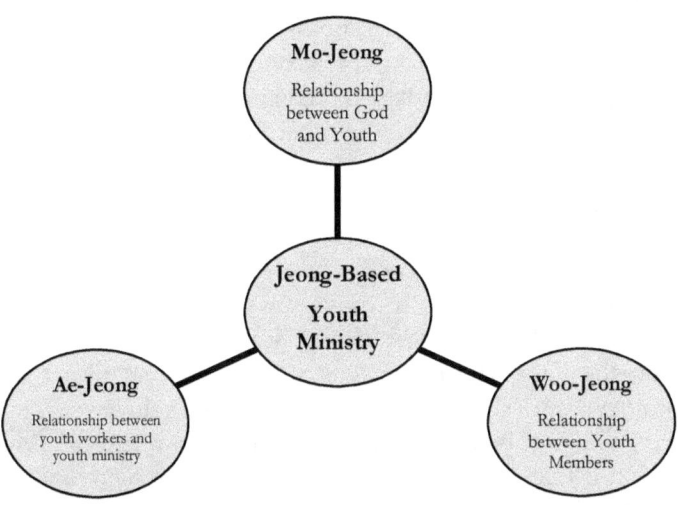

Theological Understanding of *Jeong*

In her recent book *Heart of the Cross*, Korean American theologian Wonhee Anne Joh offers the most helpful theological definition of *jeong*. She argues that *jeong* is "a Korean way of conceiving an often complex constellation of relationality of the self with the other that is deeply associated with compassion, love, vulnerability, and acceptance of heterogeneity as essential to life."[47] By examining the word *jeong* (情)[48] in its Chinese written characters,

---

[47] Wonhee Anne Joh, *Heart of the Cross: A Postcolonial Christology*, (Louisville, Kentucky: Westminster John Knox Press, 2006), xxi.
[48] The concept of *jeong* exists in Chinese, Japanese, and Korean cultures. Although their understanding of this word is subtly different, these nations use the same Chinese character of this word *jeong* (情). Thus, studying the original root of Korean word *jeong*

51

Joh discovers that *jeong* is made of three Chinese words: heart, clarity, and vulnerability.[49] Her theological exploration of *jeong* starts with the "vulnerability" part of this word. She argues that "vulnerability," along with "compassion" and "love," makes *jeong* such a valuable relational concept among Koreans. Joh affirms that "*jeong* is the power embodied in redemptive relationships."[50] *Jeong* makes a person vulnerable to the other, but this is exactly why it has a redemptive power as well.

Applying this concept of *jeong* to Christ, Joh argues that Christ's *jeong* toward the people made him vulnerable, which ultimately led to his crucifixion. It is Jesus' profound *jeong* for the world that empowers him to move toward the Cross. In the end, however, it is this *jeong* that finally heals the broken relationship between the Creator and the creation. Joh concludes that "our Christology can shift away from salvation through sacrificial suffering and can become a salvation based on relational power of *jeong*."[51] It is this relational power of *jeong* that I hope to apply to the youth ministry context.

One can simply replace the word *jeong* with "love" in Joh's theological presentation to make her overall thesis very similar to the traditional doctrine of love. Koreans, however, understand *jeong* as a much more powerful notion than love.[52] The concept of marriage offers a good example. Similar to other cultures in the world, dating and marriage are always associated with some sort of love in Korean culture. The power to sustain their marriage, however, is not love but uniquely *jeong*. By living together as a married couple, their *jeong* offers the strength to sustain their

---

(정) in Chinese character reveals the original usage of the word *jeong*. In general, this Chinese character of *jeong* offers a fundamental starting point for the meaning of *jeong* in Korean culture.
[49] Ibid, 120.
[50] Ibid, xxi.
[51] Ibid, 128
[52] The Korean translation for love is "*sarang*." Similar to the English word, *sarang* is used as both noun and verb in Korean language. For example, "I love you" = "**sarang-hae**", or "God is love" = "*hananeem-eun **sarang**-yi-ra*" In contrast, *jeong* is always used in noun form.

marriage even if they do not "feel" the love anymore. The longer they live together as a married couple, the stronger "staying power" is established through "sticky" *jeong*. "Stickiness" is one of the most popular expressions in Korean culture to describe deeper *jeong* between people.[53] When people say their *jeong* is "sticky," it means their *jeong* is very deep and their trusting relationship has built over a long time of period. The time they spent together thus plays a significant role for *jeong*.

The common expression for *jeong* among Koreans further distinguishes *jeong* from a general notion of love. Koreans say "*jeong deulda*" to express their good standing relationship with one another, which literally means "I am possessed by *jeong*" or "*jeong* has permeated or tamed me." While English language may express "I feel love" or "I give my love to you," Koreans hardly ever say "I feel *jeong*" or "I give my *jeong* to you." *Jeong* to Koreans often has more power and control over their own will. Whereas one may end or replace his/her love for another lovable person or object, *jeong* often cannot be easily ceased or substituted by one's own power.

The meaning of divorce in the Korean culture further elucidates such a power of *jeong*. In the Western culture, divorce can be viewed as the end of one relationship and possibly the beginning of the next. The marriage relationship may end with divorce, but it is possible to sustain or transform a couple's relationship into a friendship. This progressive idea of a transformational relationship does not seem to fit in Korean sentiment. The concept of keeping a relationship with one's ex-wife or ex-husband is therefore a rough and a strange concept to many Koreans. *Jeong* does not allow for such a phenomenon. The initial cause of the divorce may vary, but the consequence of such a broken marriage relationship is always the end of *jeong*. When *jeong* is gone, Koreans say "*jeong ddul-uh-jee-da*" (opposite to "*jeong-deul-da*"), which can be literally translated as "*jeong* has dropped [from my heart]." Once this happened, it is extremely difficult to have any relationship with the person with whom one had previous *jeong* at all. Generally speaking, there is no such thing as ex-wife or ex-husband as a relational concept in

---

[53] Wonhee Anne Joh, *Heart of the Cross: A Postcolonial Christology*, 121.

Korean culture. The relationship ends. The "dropped" *jeong* does not allow both parties to co-exist in the same place. *Jeong* has power in Korean culture both positively and negatively. It must be, therefore, handled with exceptional care in the youth ministry context.

Although my application of *jeong* for youth ministry involves mainly positive outcomes, the negative consequences of it must be also addressed. As I presented in the previous paragraph, *Jeong* has its double-edgedness which can create and destroy relationships. When *jeong* is employed properly in youth ministry, the youth members and their pastor can experience "sticky" *jeong* among themselves which will offer "staying power" to further build a healthy community in Christ. On the other hand, however, there exists this dangerous side of *jeong* which can fatally destroy a community. Youth ministers therefore must remember that if *jeong* is treated carelessly or abused in a wrong way in a KA youth context, the damage will be enormous.[54] *Jeong* makes a person vulnerable. *Jeong* can offer a "sticky" bonding relationship; at the same time because of its absolute openness, one can also be susceptible to receiving tremendous hurt. Therefore, it must be handled with special care. This vulnerability of *jeong*, however, can offer a powerful trust and relational space in youth ministry if one can understand and employ *jeong* sincerely with others.

Three Dimensions of Jeong: Becoming a Jeong-sharer

Although there are many different dimensions of *jeong*, the common underlying foundation of the concept of *jeong* is relationship. No matter how this word is used, it is used in a context of describing a relationship between something or, more often, someone. This relationship in which *jeong* is embedded,

---

[54] I will discuss about the problem of abusing *jeong* in the KA context in the Theology of the Cross section of this paper. *Jeong* is a human concept derived from experiences; therefore, it can be abused. Using a KA teenage girl, Bin-Na's story, I will further discuss about the abusive case of *jeong* in KA context and how the message of the Cross can redeem *jeong* from such an abusive case.

however, has a special characteristic of fully giving oneself to the other. Andrew Root's reading of Dietrich Bonheoffer's concept of relationship comes very close to the concept of *jeong*:

> Therefore, for Bonhoeffer, relationships are not simply about earning leverage for influence, but rather about sharing in each other's existence, in each other's suffering, as one shares in the other's place (*Stellvertretung*) and in so doing stands with Christ.[55]

In his article *Reexamining Relational Youth Ministry: Implications from the Theology of Bonhoeffer*, Andrew Root offers a valuable argument for the importance of relational youth ministry based on place-sharing and not on influence. The concept of a "place-sharing" relationship offers a crucial insight for understanding the concept of *jeong*. Using Bonhoeffer's theology, Root argues that "place-sharing happens when one places himself or herself fully in the reality of the other, refusing to turn away even from its horror."[56] Our willingness to fully share the place of another in spite of "its horror" or the moments of self-sacrifice makes our relationship truly Christian. This describes well the spirit of *jeong*. It allows youth members to be this kind of radical "place-sharer," who can be fully present with the other even if there is a risk of self-sacrifice. I will expand this component of "self-sacrifice" in *jeong* at three different levels: 1) *woo-jeong* between youth to youth, 2) *ae-jeong* from youth pastor/worker to youth members, and 3) *mo-jeong* from God to youth members.

Woo-jeong between Youth members: Staying Power as Friends

The concept of *jeong* always includes a risk-taking factor due to its vulnerability component. Especially in the concept of *woo-jeong*

---

[55] Andrew Root, *Word and World* volume 26, Number 3, summer 2006, 270.
[56] Root, 274.

(friendship), the risk-taking and self-sacrifice factor has been always portrayed as one of the highest friendship characteristics in Korean culture. The special term for such sacrificial expectation between friends is called *ui-ri* (의리), which means loyalty, integrity, or obligation. If one has a true *woo-jeong* with another, that person will expect unconditional *ui-ri* from his or her friend, even if that means losing one's life. In the Korean culture, *ui-ri* is greatly valued and expected. One can easily find such phenomenon in many Korean movies and in T.V. dramas.[57] Almost every Korean movie has ingredients of emphasizing *ui-ri* between two friends. In the end of the movies, either one friend dies for the other or both friends with strong *ui-ri* die together for the sake of their *woo-jeong*.[58]

According to the concept of *ui-ri*, this kind of commitment requires no validation, logic, or reason. Friends with *ui-ri* can die for each other for the sake of their *woo-jeong* with or without any logical explanation. Thus, when Koreans make *jeong*-related commitments, they become a strong cohesive group bonded by *jeong* which produces a dependable community.[59] I suspect that this may explain a reason for the notable growth of Christianity in Korean

---

[57] Wonhee A. Joh also mentioned one Korean movie (*Joint Security Area*) to explain the existence of *jeong* even between North and South Korean soldiers. Even though they were enemies in terms of their uniform, they were able to build *woo-jeong* to the point where one could die for the other. The scene that describes the death for the friend for the sake of their *woo-jeong* is very common in popular Korean movies.

[58] Interestingly, the message of *ui-ri* in Korean Media is not only influential to those who are living in Korea. Through the advance of media technology and rise of high interest of their motherland, many Korean American youths are also exposed to such a message. Even though many of them cannot fully comprehend the Korean movies due to language and cultural differences, they seem to identify the message of the *woo-jeong* correctly. The concept of *ui-ri* seems to appear as a "cool thing" among KA teenagers who watched the Korean movies.

[59] Obviously, the side effect for such community could be exclusiveness of their membership. For those who don't share *jeong* with them, they cannot be fully integrated into this community. Youth pastors, therefore, must be careful not to make a cohesive youth group too exclusive. The focus of creating a cohesive community of Christ through *jeong* is to offer the staying power in Christ with full openness to anyone who would like to join. *Jeong* does not promote exclusiveness of membership. It can, however, certainly lead members of the community to be exclusive to the others.

culture. When Koreans heard the message of Jesus in John 15:13, "greater love has no one than this, that he lay down his life for his friends," they could have easily related this friendship message with the concept of *ui-ri*. Many Korean Christians not only became followers of Christ, but *woo-jeong*-sharers with Christ, who have made their commitment in response to Christ's *jeong*, who died for them as a friend on the Cross.

This concept of *woo-jeong* creates "staying power" in our youth context to build an authentic and radical community of Jesus Christ. This attempt of doing "friendship ministry" in youth groups is not a new idea in contemporary youth ministries, but *woo-jeong* requires a radical commitment. The goal of sharing *woo-jeong* is not only to gather youth members to a church through friendship, but to build *ui-ri* among youth members to share their lives together. This *ui-ri* demands that each youth member be available to one another even if that means sacrificing one's own success and time. Friends with this *ui-ri* truly "refuse to turn away even from its horror."

The friendship between David and Jonathan offers a good *woo-jeong* and *ui-ri* model for youth ministry. Even though their status was radically different, one being king Saul's enemy and the other being the son of the king, their *woo-jeong* offered "staying power" for both. Jonathan's *ui-ri* was clearly expressed through allowing David to run away from King Saul, which was an act of direct disobedience to his father. On the other hand, David's *ui-ri* was kept, even after Jonathan's death, by offering kindness to Jonathan's family. In this story, neither of them died for his friend, but their *woo-jeong* saved David's life first, and then Jonathan's whole family later. Both friends did not refuse their *woo-jeong* even at the times of trouble. Jonathan's *woo-jeong* was able to offer "staying power" with David, which in return resulted in the safety of Jonathan's family even after Jonathan's death.

Teaching the value of *woo-jeong* between David and Jonathan is a challenging task in any youth ministry. It is especially difficult in KA context where teenagers' freedom to sacrifice is restricted by their parents who control the most of their daily schedules. With the exception of youth retreats or mission trip days, youth members do not have much choice to keep *ui-ri* with their friends. It is very difficult for the youth to share their place with the others without getting help from their parents, since in many cases, youth cannot drive by themselves. Moreover, the fact that Korean churches are not local churches to almost all members makes such effort to share *woo-jeong* during weekdays even more intricate.

The busy life style of contemporary teenagers further limits their freedom to share suffering with friends. They are extremely busy with their studies and extra-curricular activities in a highly success-driven society. In order to survive and achieve the highest academic success, many youth are packed with daily lessons and tutoring. For many of the KA youth in this society, success unfortunately seems to take its priority over friendship. Academic achievements are valued as superior to *woo-jeong*. Our competitive materialistic social system allows no time for the youth to have a radical *woo-jeong* relationship with other members in a community.

Jesus' community of faith, however, is radically different. This is why youth pastors who strive to teach the gospel of Jesus Christ must continue to encourage the youth and parents to understand the significance of building *woo-jeong* in the midst of such resistance. This community of Jesus Christ does not prioritize personal success over other members of the body. The church of Christ does not ignore suffering members due to busy schedules. The message of the Kingdom of God from Jesus Christ is clear. In the midst of busy life in this world, teenagers must learn to stop for those who need their presence. The life and ministry of Jesus Christ proves such a point. Jesus stopped for the beggars, the poor, the demon-possessed, and the marginalized members of society who needed *woo-jeong* of Jesus. As followers of Christ, youth pastors must continue to teach the youth to be a part of this Kingdom movement of Jesus. The body of Christ cannot live well while other parts of body are experiencing pain.

The role of *woo-jeong*, therefore, is not only to be morally "nice" to one another, but to be radically available to one another in the midst of busy schedule. Bonheoffer is clearly right that, "the physical presence of other Christians is a source of incomparable joy and strength to the believer."⁶⁰ Through the concept of *woo-jeong* they will share their joys and sufferings as one body of Christ. Through *ui-ri* between the friends, the youth may sacrifice their "success" for other's needs. Through their sacrifice for one another, they will understand the true *woo-jeong* of Jesus Christ, who expressed the greatest love by dying on the cross for his friends. Through *ui-ri* among teenagers in a community of Christ, I even hope that their parents can also rediscover the value of their *woo-jeong* with other adult members in the congregation.

Ae-jeong of Youth Pastor

If *woo-jeong* among youth members can create a radical "staying power" among youth members, it is the concept of *ae-jeong* that gives "staying power" for youth pastors to stay in their ministry. Lack of *ae-jeong* for either youth members or youth ministry is the leading cause of many young first-year youth pastors to leave the youth ministry. *Ae-jeong* at the basic level means a special affection towards something. If a youth pastor loses that affection towards youth members and/or youth ministry itself, no right relationship can be established. It is evident that in the course of the youth ministry experience, youth ministers will face many difficult challenges. In times of such difficult moments, youth pastors' *ae-jeong* to their own flock of adolescents will provide the "staying power" to continue their ministries. Simon Peter's story of denial (John 18) and Jesus' reinstatement of Peter (John 21) offers the best *ae-jeong* model for youth pastors in Korean American churches. Even though Peter failed to keep his *woo-jeong* with Jesus, the resurrected Christ's *ae-jeong* bestows restoration of the broken relationship with Peter. Peter's dramatic denial of his *woo-jeong* with Christ did not stop Jesus from calling him back. Throughout the course of youth ministry, youth pastors will face resistance and denial of *woo-jeong* from both youth members and their parents. In

---

⁶⁰ Dietrich Bonhoeffer, *Life Together*, 19.

the midst of such despair, *ae-jeong* will offer enduring energy of "staying power" for youth pastors to stay faithful in their calling.

The Korean word *ae-jeong* contains two distinct meanings, and the combination of those two definitions offers the constructive concept of *ae-jeong* to youth pastors. The first meaning of *ae-jeong* contains the connotation of compassion, a feeling of sorrow, grief, and pity towards a person or a group of people.[61] The gospel writers' portrayal of Jesus' compassionate heart offers the best translation of this *ae-jeong*. The aspect of *ae-jeong* from Jesus towards the people around him is clearly apparent throughout his ministry. Especially from the Gethsemane to the cross, Jesus was full of sorrow and grief not only due to his physical suffering, but also for the unbelieving generations around him. While watching his disciples fall asleep on the Mount of Olives (Luke 22:45), while witnessing Judas and Peter disown him in front of the crowd, and even while dying on the cross, Jesus' *ae-jeong* for the people around him was clearly sketched by the gospel writers. Jesus' prayer on the cross expresses his *ae-jeong* even at the moment of death, "Father forgive them for they do not know what they are dong" (Luke 23:34). While every one of his friends was forfeiting their *woo-jeong* with Jesus, his *ae-jeong* still sought for their forgiveness. While every follower of Christ denied his ministry, he faithfully stayed at his course to finish the Kingdom work that he had started. Youth pastors of today may also have to face the same lonely and frustrated moments through the course of the service. While *woo-jeong* from the youth members can be denied by them, the *ae-jeong* for the adolescents will assist the youth pastor to stay the course in continuing the Kingdom work.

Jesus' breakfast story with his disciples in John 21 presents the second facet of *ae-jeong*. With the first aspect of *ae-jeong* in his heart, Jesus conducts a breakfast meeting by offering bread and fish

---

[61] In Korean, there is only one word *ae-jeong* (애정) to expresses two different meanings. In Chinese, however, there are two distinct characters (哀情) and (愛情) for each meaning. Since the Korean word *ae-jeong* is originated from Chinese character, it is helpful to see two different Chinese characters to understand the deeper meaning of this word for those who know Chinese.

to his unfaithful disciples. The disciples, on the other hand of course, could not speak a word to their Lord who was being merciful to them. It was Jesus' compassionate heart that invited the disciples to the table. This mood of sadness, however, transforms into a mood of love through another *ae-jeong* of Jesus. When they had finished eating, Jesus asked, "Do you love me?" three times not only to confirm Peter's love to Jesus, but Jesus' love to Peter. The second aspect of *ae-jeong* means affection and tender feeling towards a person with whom one previously had a meaningful relationship.

This affectionate feeling is uniquely strong because of the previous relationships. It is in this *ae-jeong* that Jesus forgives and reclaims Peter and his disciples. Neither Peter's denial of his friendship nor the disciples' failure to be "place-sharers" with Christ was able to destroy Jesus' love for his disciples. It is this second aspect of *ae-jeong* that made the disciples precious treasures to Christ. By asking three "love" questions, Jesus affirmed his profound *ae-jeong* to his disciples. Jesus' compassionate heart (first *ae-jeong*) allowed for the disciples to return to Jesus; at the same time the affectionate heart of Jesus (second *ae-jeong*) reclaimed the stickiness of their loving relationship once again. Through the first meaning of *ae-jeong*, Jesus offered forgiveness, and through the second meaning of *ae-jeong*, he expressed the gracious love of God.

Jesus was a "place-sharer" with his disciples, especially with Peter, throughout his ministry. Yet, at Jesus' critical moment where no one was sharing his suffering, Peter not only denied his discipleship in Christ, but publicly cut off his *woo-jeong* relationship with his "Christ, the Son of the living God" (Matt. 15:16). The cost of Peter's betrayal would be death to those who value *woo-jeong* vitally. The death for broken *woo-jeong*, however, came upon Christ instead. While *woo-jeong* between Peter and Jesus was destroyed by Peter's denial, Jesus' *ae-jeong* toward Peter healed the relationship. It is this two-fold dimension of *ae-jeong* that youth pastors must strive for in their ministry.

Youth pastors with this *jeong* in Korean church context, therefore, not only need to become "place-sharers," but also *ae-jeong*-sharers who are willing to suffer with and for adolescents, even those who do not seek help from their youth pastors. Teenagers may break their *woo-jeong* with the pastor from time to time, but with *ae-jeong*, pastors can offer forgiveness and love. It is necessary for youth pastors to build *woo-joeng* with the students, but they must remember that it is *ae-jeong* that keeps the relationship beyond the friendship level. Adolescents in youth ministry do not simply expect a true friendship from their pastors; rather they expect their pastors to be spiritual leaders. *Woojeong* can build strong bonds within a youth group, but the *ae-jeong* of the pastor will bring lost teenagers to the breakfast table of the Lord once again.

Mo-jeong, the *Hesed* of God

Out of all three types of *jeong*, the word *mo-jeong* is considered the most powerful and "sticky" one. At the fundamental level, it can be literally translated as *"jeong* of mother [to her own child]." It is uniquely assigned to mothers for their expression of *jeong* towards the children. From the moment of birth, mothers' *mo-jeong* towards her own child is so fervent, it cannot be found in any other relationship. It is by far more sacrificial, loving, forgiving, and "sticky" than other types of relationship, not because the child offers anything profitable to the mother, but because the child is her own. No matter what the child does, the *mo-jeong* of the mother does not change.[62] It presumes unconditional love from a mother to her child. A mother is always faithful and loving to her child. The child, in return, can grow up with a strong trusting relationship with his/her mother. The concept of *mo-jeong*, therefore, can only exist in a family wih two unequal sides, a mother who pours everything and a child who receives everything.

Unlike *woo-jeong* and *ae-jeong*, *mo-jeong* does not require any conditions. Rather, the only prerequisite to receive *mo-jeong* is to become a child. In return, the only way to practice *mo-jeong* is to

---

[62] Obviously, there are numbers of mothers who give up their child due to various reasons, thus giving up their *mo-jeong* as well. I also acknowledge that there are some irresponsible mothers who raise their child without any noticeable *mo-jeong* in her family. In general, however, I believe the majority of the mothers in this world do raise their children with sincere *mo-jeong*, and I am concerned with such *mo-jeong* of those mothers.

become a parent. The Korean proverb regarding *mo-jeong* suggests such a relationship very well: "The only way to comprehend the meaning of *mo-jeong* is to become a parent." Whereas *woo-jeong* and *ae-jeong* could fade away, the concept of *mo-jeong* encloses one's child in everlasting and absolute love. It is in this concept of *mo-jeong*, I would argue, that the love of God can be expressed more convincingly to Korean American youth. This concept of the *mo-jeong* of God thus offers another "staying power" in youth ministry: the power to stay in relationship with God. The *mo-jeong* of God will always provide an opportunity for God's children to have a deeper relationship with God. At the same time, "like a mother who will not forsake her nursing child, like a father who runs to welcome the prodigal home"[63] God's *mo-jeong* will never give up on God's own children.

Although Jesus tends to describe God's love as a Father's love in the New Testament, Yahweh's love to Israel in the Old Testaments depicts more of the concept of *mo-jeong*. The relationship between Israelites and their God, Yahweh, reveals an excellent example of mo-*jeong*. Throughout the Old Testament, the love of God to Israel has been expressed through various stories. From the stories of Moses to the Minor Prophets, the faithfulness (*Hesed*) of God's love in the midst of the unfaithful Israelites controls the history of Israel.

The Hebrew word *hesed* offers a helpful resource to understand the concept of *mo-jeong*. Many scholars agree that word *hesed* is exceptionally difficult to render into English. Such a difficulty of translating *hesed* into English is evident in the various Biblical translations. The word *hesed* in Hosea 6:6 has been translated as "mercy" (KJV), "steadfast love" (NRSV), "goodness" (JPSV), and "loyalty" (REB). [64] In general, the above four descriptions convey the common meaning of *hesed*. Katharine Sakenfeld's book, *The Meaning of Hesed in Hebrew Bible*, however, offers a helpful theological explanation of the word *hesed*. According to Sakenfeld, the word *hesed* is used in relationships that

---

[63] PCUSA, *The Book of Confession*, A Brief Statement of Faith.
[64] Bernhard W. Anderson, *Understanding the Old Testament*, 277-8.

exist between two unequal sides.[65] The weaker or needy side seeks *hesed* from the stronger and resourceful side. Bernhard Anderson also confirms that *hesed* seems "to apply to relationships in which one party is 'superior' in the sense of having more power or influence by virtue of social position."[66] God to the Israelites was always a "superior" party who supplied everything they needed even at the moment when the Israelites betrayed their God. It is this stronger side of the party who offered a continuation of the relationship in the midst of the denial of the weaker side. This applies to the concept of *mo-jeong*. Even though a child, a weaker and inferior side, denies the relationship, the mother never gives up on her child and continues to offer mercy, goodness, loyalty, and steadfast love.

In the Deuteronomic tradition, *hesed* is also associated with *berit* (convenant).[67] *Hesed* is employed as an important concept which enables God to continue God's special relationships with the people who broke the covenant. God, the faithful mother or father, redeems them not on the basis of the doctrine of works-righteousness, but by that of *hesed*. This is the doctrine of grace. By the grace of God, the unholy people of Israel could continue to have their relationship with the holy God. As Sakenfeld argues,

> The term *hesed* thus proves to be one which throughout the tradition was remarkably rich in its theological meaning. Here the sovereign freedom of God and his strong commitment to his chosen people were held together in a single word. A single word expressed the utter dependence of the people upon Yahweh and his willingness and ability to deliver them.[68]

---

[65] Katharine D. Sakenfeld, *The Meaning of Hesed in the Hebrew Bible: A New Inquiry*.
[66] Anderson, *Understanding the Old testament*, 278.
[67] Sakenfeld, 82-90, 133-35.
[68] Ibid., 238.

Similar to the concept of *mo-jeong*, the ancient writers of the Scriptures wished to convey the relational "staying power" between God and God's chosen children, the Israelites, in this single word *hesed*.[69]

In the New Testament, God's *mo-jeong* reaches its highest point at the cross. God's *mo-jeong* to his only son is very disturbing because God allowed his "only son" to suffer and die on the cross. What kind of *mo-jeong* allows an only child to suffer and die? This troubling incident of the cross makes the concept of *mo-jeong* much more complex, yet profound. Through this tragic event, God opened the door of God's relationship to all humanity. The *mo-jeong* of God is not only limited to the Israelites, but is available to all children of God. In fact, God's *mo-jeong* is extended to the whole creation. This extension is possible because of the cross, which expressed God's *mo-jeong* at its highest pinnacle. It is not only the human Jesus who died on the cross, but the divine Jesus as well. God through Jesus, taking man's place, also suffered and experienced a human death on the cross for us. Just like any mother would risk her own life to save her child, God took the path of the cross to demonstrate God's own *mo-jeong* for us: "while we were still sinners, Christ died for us" (Rom. 5:8). On the cross, God both extended and expressed God's *mo-jeong* for all humankind.

In this concept of *hesed* or *mo-jeong* of God, adolescents can gain two crucial lessons in regard to having a relationship with God. First, the *mo-jeong* of God assures a loving relationship between God (the parent) and the youth members (God's children). Like the father who waits for his prodigal son, God's relationship is always available to the youth because God's *mo-jeong* is stronger than anything else in this universe (Romans 8:38-39). Second, this relationship with God is totally based on God's grace. Having a

---

[69] Sakenfeld's summary of theological use of *hesed* in Deuteronomic tradition further explains the profundity of the word: "Thus we may say that *hesed* was a particularly useful word for peaking of God's relationship to his people, collectively and individually, because it held together in a single expression as emphasis on divine freedom on the one hand and divine commitment on the other, an emphasis on divine power on the one hand and divine care on the other, an emphasis on human need and weakness on the one hand and human responsibility to trust in God alone on the other" (Sakenfeld, 149).

relationship with God is radically different than any other human relationship. This special relationship with God is offered by God toward God's creation, not because of our worthiness, but because of God's grace. Anderson gets it right when he writes, "*Hesed* is an act of inner faithfulness and therefore of grace."[70] Through this concept of God's *mo-jeong*, youth members will experience a deeper and "sticky" relationship of grace with God.

The *mo-jeong* of God further strengthens a youth group to share their *jeong* with one another because of God who is *jeong*. 1 John 4 explains it well:

> Dear friends, let us [share *jeong* with] one another, for [*jeong*] comes from God… This is how God showed his [*jeong*] among us: He sent his one and only Son into the world that we might live through him. This is [*jeong*]; not that we [shared *woo-jeong* or *ae-jeong* with] God, but that he [offered *mo-jeong* to] us and sent his Son as an atoning sacrifice for our sins. Dear friends, since God [shared *jeong* with] us, we also ought to [share *jeong* with] one another (1 John 4:7-11).

We share *jeong* with one another because God first shared God's *mo-jeong* with us. The youth ministry that strives to share *jeong* must start from here.

Jeong-Based Youth Ministry

Through three types of *jeong*, I have explained three different "staying powers" in three different relationships. *Woo-jeong* provides a strong bond between youth members (including a youth pastor) to build a genuine community of Christ, whose members can sacrifice their time and goods for one another. *Ae-jeong* empowers youth pastors to stay the course of youth ministry even

---

[70] Anderson, 278.

in times of trial and burden. Having a special *ae-jeong* toward youth members and ministry itself will support youth pastors in continuing their faithful kingdom work. Lastly, the concept of *mo-jeong* delivers profound relational treasures regarding our relationship with God. Similar in concept with *hesed*, God' *mo-jeong* will graciously offer a sacred relationship with God to God's own children.

In his helpful book *Life Together*, Dietrich Bonhoeffer opens his first chapter with Psalm 133:1, "Behold, how good and how pleasant it is for brethren to dwell together in unity."[71] With this scripture, Bonhoeffer expands the beauty of sharing life together under the Word of God. At the end of his chapter, however, Bonhoeffer concludes that dwelling together must be done through Christ, "for Jesus Christ alone is our unity."[72] I strongly agree with Bonhoeffer that any type of Christian community, including the youth group, must dwell through Christ and Christ alone. The concept of *jeong* is not against this ultimate goal of Christian community. Rather, the theology of *jeong* plays as a "sticky" instrument for youth groups to dwell together for Jesus Christ. Clearly, Jesus alone provides the ultimate cause of Christian gathering. The concept and practice of *jeong* in the KA context supports this cause to be more efficient in its own cultural background. Through Christ's friendship stories in the gospel, the youth members can understand the true meaning of *woo-jeong* among themselves. Through Christ's *ae-jeong* towards his own flock, the youth pastors can regain the pastoral passion to stay strong and faithful in the ministry. Finally, through the death of Christ on the Cross, both youth members and pastors can be confident about God's *mo-jeong*, God's "sticky" unconditional love and grace, in their lives.

Youth pastors who hope to cultivate *jeong*-based ministry must remember that the community of *jeong*-sharers is built upon the body and not upon the word. The fourth evangelist testifies, "the Word became flesh and made his dwelling among us" (John

---

[71] Bonheoffer, 17.
[72] Ibid, 39.

1:14). *Jeong* cannot be simply shared through youth pastors' teaching, reading, writing or speaking of it. Rather, *jeong* can be only shared through feeding, cleaning, touching, and holding between the members of the community, as Jesus did throughout his ministry. Through Jesus' feeding of the crowds, cleaning and washing of his disciples' feet, touching the sick and the dead, and holding the children, Jesus' *jeong* penetrated into people's heart. Youth pastors must to follow such actions of Jesus. Saint Francis' message sums up the core lesson of building the *jeong*-based youth ministry, "preach the gospel, if necessary use words."

CHAPTER FIVE

PRACTICAL TOOLS FOR
THE FIRST YEAR YOUTH PASTOR

I learned most of my teaching and discipline skills through my graduate teaching credential program and three years of high school teaching experience. The teaching credential program trained me well enough to boldly finish the first year of my teaching assignment at Hoover high school. I struggled and made countless mistakes; yet I managed to survive my first year and made greater progress in my second and third year of teaching. After finishing my third year at Hoover high, I moved on to study theology at seminary because I had a greater passion for Christian education in a church setting. I wanted to apply public teaching tools into church so the children and youth could learn about God and the Christian faith in the most effective way. Although I am still in process of learning, the four years of my seminary experience offered sufficient theological education for me to see various connections between the public school educational system and children and youth ministry. I would like to share some of my teaching tools that have been effectively used to teach faith to the younger generations. Especially for those who had no previous formal teaching experience and training, I hope to introduce some of the useful teaching and discipline tools to help youth pastors become effective teachers of the faith.

The first tool is what I call the Ministry Standards for Youth Pastors (MSYP) in KA context. The MSYP is sort of the youth pastors' version of the California Standards for the Teaching Profession (CSTP) that I learned in the teaching credential program.[73] CSTP offered a self evaluation rubric for my teaching profession, which I enabled me to honestly assess my teaching performance. It was like a mirror that helped me to honestly reflect on my teaching performances. For first year teachers, such reflective and evaluative standards are absolutely necessary because they do not know what to expect from the students as well as their teaching performances. CSTP presented many crucial guides for becoming an effective teacher for me. I see similar needs for first year children and youth pastors. We need some sort of professional standards that can guide and mirror our faith teaching "performances."[74] Using CSTP as the basic framework, I propose MSYP as the mirror for pastors who are trying to teach the Word of God to youths.

The second set of tools that I would like to recommend are the basic teaching and discipline tools that I learned from Harry and Rosemary Wong's book, *The First Days of School*.[75] As the title of the book suggests, the authors' argument is clear: that the first days of school are extremely critical for teachers. Unfortunately, however, only a few teachers (and youth pastors as well) get any experience or training during student teaching to prepare for such an important

---

[73] I am indebted to the ideas from the California Standards for the Teaching Profession (CSTP), which has been adopted by the California Department of Education. The overall framework of my Standards for the Youth Pastors is based on the CSTP (www.ctc.ca.gov/reports/cstpreport.pdf).

[74] Although our youth ministry duties cannot and should not be just a "performance," I do believe we need to evaluate our services as youth pastors/ministers/teachers. Without such evaluation of our actions or "performances," no improvement can be expected.

[75] Harry Wong and Rosemary Wong, *The First Days of School: How to Be an Effective Teacher*, 1998.

day. Wong suggests that, "what happens on the first days of school will be an accurate indicator of your success for the rest of the school year." [76] Although the youth ministry setting is quite different than the public school setting, I see the same need for youth pastors to prepare for their first weeks of ministry well since both public school teachers and youth pastors face the same age groups. These adolescents know whether the new teacher or new pastor is ready for their job or not on the first day. The first Lord's Day worship services or the first Bible study classes for new youth pastors, therefore, is critical in their ministry because that first impression will last for a long time. Similarly, the first Lord's Day for a new school calendar year matters as well.[77] For those who are planning to start their first youth ministry or wish to have a better academic year, Wong's book will be a helpful guide to start the first day of ministry with many effective teaching and discipline techniques for children and youth pastors.

Ministry Standards for Youth Pastors (MSYT)

The Ministry Standards for Youth Pastors in a Korean-American Context provide a common language and a practical tool for cultivating organic faith in a Korean American youth ministry setting. These Standards are based on the five catechetical principles of Deuteronomy and the concept and practice of *jeong*, which I have explored in the previous chapters. The Standards are to be used by youth pastors to prompt reflection about their teaching and learning, develop professional goals, and guide, monitor, and evaluate the progress of youth pastors' ministry-related practices toward faithful goals. The Standards address the unique difficulties of teaching and practicing the Christian faith in Korean American churches today and reflect a holistic view of faith teaching for children and adolescents.

---

[76] Wong and Wong, *The First Days of School*, 3.
[77] The new school calendar year usually happens during July or September where new groups of youth members, such as 9th grade for Sr. high ministry and 6 or 7th graders for Jr. High, move into the ministry.

There are six standards that can guide new youth pastors to be effective and faithful youth workers in the Korean-American church setting. Since youth ministry is not a profession in which a single approach or method can be effective for all pastors and youth groups, youth pastors have to creatively adapt the Standards in their own unique setting. Although I respect the diverse ways in which each youth pastor pursues a faithful serving of a youth ministry, these Standards will articulate a common and basic level of teaching. The Standards are organized around six interrelated principles. The six standards are:

1) Theologically-Centered Teaching: Understanding and Organizing Theology for Youth Learning.
2) Humanly-Adaptable Teaching: Planning Instruction and Designing Faith Experiences for All Youths
3) Generation-Inclusive Teaching: Engaging and Supporting All Members of Youth Ministry in Learning
4) Socially-Transformative Teaching: Assessing and Applying Youths Learning in Their Lives
5) Communally-Oriented Teaching: Creating and Maintaining Effective Environments for Community of Jesus Christ
6) *Jeong*-Based Teaching: Developing as a *Jeong*-Sharing Educator/Teacher/ Counselor/Pastor.

Again, these six standards address only a sample of the important facets of teaching faith in a youth ministry setting, and do not represent all the possible issues or aspects of youth ministry. The Standards, however, are a useful framework for a new youth pastor. They will not make anyone into an expert on Korean-American youth ministry. Rather, the Standards will support new youth pastors in a Korean-American church setting by providing direction for their ministry journey.

I strongly recommend using these standards to reflect and evaluate youth pastors' own faith teachings in various youth ministry activities: The Lord's Day worship, small group bible studies, retreats, lock-ins, fellowship meetings, leadership training, mission trips, etc. No youth group meeting or program can be wasted because every moment with adolescents is precisely and urgently a teaching moment. Reflecting upon these standards can help a youth pastor to make thoughtful and faithful decisions about instructional strategies to passionately and effectively pass on the faith to youth members.

> # STANDARD ONE
> UNDERSTANDING AND ORGANIZING THEOLOGICAL TEACHING
> FOR YOUTH LEARNING
> *(THEOLOGICALLY-CENTERED TEACHING)*

Objective: Youth pastors exhibit a strong working knowledge of Christian Theology and the Bible. Youth pastors organize curriculum to facilitate students' understanding of the central doctrines of Christian theology and the main themes of the Bible. Youth pastors interrelate various biblical books (both OT and NT) to extend youth members' understanding and practice of faith.

Key Questions to Ask: As youth pastors develop, they should ask, "How or why do I..."

1) ensure that my knowledge of the Bible and the Christian theology is sufficient to support youth members' learning about the triune God?
2) continue to keep my theological knowledge current?
3) use my theological knowledge to organize a curriculum that will increase youth members understanding?
4) organize curriculum according to youth members' levels (both age and theological knowledge) to ensure that each member develops a deep understanding of core concepts of the Bible?[78]
5) challenge all youth members' to think critically when they read the Word of God?
6) help all youth members develop passion for and a deep knowledge of the Bible and the basic Christian theology?
7) build on youth members life experience, prior knowledge, and interests to make the Bible and theology relevant and meaningful in their spiritual lives?

Youth group is a serious place. Youth members come to church to enjoy God and glorify God together. It is a place of worship and a place to learn the Bible. If youth just want fun, they will go to a party, the beach, a movie, or shopping. They come to youth group because it is a church. Therefore, any types of youth activities must be theologically centered and never cease to proclaim the Word of God in a youth church.

---

[78] I found James Fowler's *Stage of Faith* a very helpful resource to understand different stages of faith for a human being. Fowler's developmental faith theory will guide a youth pastor to appropriately adjust their faith teaching lesson for different age groups. I also find James Loder's *The Logic of the Spirit* as complimentary resource to Fowler. Loder acknowledges that psychological stage theories enable us to recognize the development of human understanding. At the same time, he argues that the Holy Spirit has its own developmental logic that is not bound by stages. Both Fowler and Loder offer a good balance between psychological and spiritual stages of the faith development of youth.

STANDARD TWO
PLANNING INSTRUCTION AND DESIGNING FAITH EXPERIENCE
FOR ALL YOUTH MEMBERS
(HUMANLY-ADAPTABLE TEACHING)

Objectives: Youth pastors plan faith instruction that draws on and values youths' spiritual background, prior biblical knowledge, and interests. Youth pastors use various teaching aids (music, drama, arts, and other multi-media tools) in their worship services and other teaching gatherings to accommodate cultural needs among today's youths. This involves designing long-term and short-term lesson plans to balance different instructional activities that promote youths' participation. Youth pastors modify and adjust instructional plans according to youth engagement and their unique needs.

Key Questions to Ask: As youth pastors develop, they should ask, "How or why do I…"

1) recognize and incorporate youths' diverse interests and needs into worship services and Bible studies?
2) design the Lord's Day worship service so that newcomers (both Christian and non-Christian) can engage in worship?
3) adjust the lesson plan to make the theological teaching relevant and accessible to each youth member's life?
4) modify my plans to ensure opportunities for all youth members to learn and practice faith teachings?
5) choose and adapt Bible study materials which address the major concerns of today's youth (such as study, sex, relationships, family matters, violence, drugs, alcohol, etc.)?
6) develop short-term and long-term plans that build on and extend youths' understanding of the Bible and Christian theology?
7) change my teaching styles so I can be more flexible yet faithful in preaching the gospel?

Becoming a flexible youth pastor never means becoming a popular pastor among youth members by adapting to everything they want. The goal of this standard is to modify and design youth ministry so the message of Jesus Christ can be effectively delivered to contemporary youths. Incorporating diverse methods in worship services or Bible studies, therefore, is needed for the sake of the unchangeable message of the gospel.

STANDARD THREE
ENGAGING AND SUPPORTING ALL YOUTH MINISTRY RELATED MEMBERS, INCLUDING PARENTS AND TEACHERS
(GENERATION- INCLUSIVE TEACHING)

Objective: Youth pastors build their youth program not only on youths, but on their families and volunteer teachers. Youth pastors use a variety of instructional strategies and resources to support parents in becoming spiritual teachers for their child. Youth pastors also engage and support adult volunteers to be effective and caring small group leaders for youths. Youth pastors actively engage both parents and teachers to have the same instructional goal for youth members. Youth pastors assist both parents and adult volunteers in becoming self-directed spiritual teachers.

Key Questions to Ask: As youth pastors develop, they should ask, "How or why do I..."

1) inspire parents to initiate their spiritual parenting role in their family setting?
2) encourage all parents of youths to consider themselves as a part of youth ministry?
3) provide opportunities (PTA, parents' seminar, teachers' seminar) for parents and teachers to think, discuss, interact, reflect, and evaluate both youth ministry and their role in it?
4) help all volunteer teachers be faithful in their roles?
5) explain the role of parents and teachers in their faith learning experiences?
6) motivate youth members to have a spiritual conversation with their parents at home?
7) support the whole family to be lifetime prayer partners for one another?

Engaging and supporting parents and adult volunteer teachers are the toughest parts of youth ministry. Not only it is difficult to gather all parents in one place or recruit responsible volunteers, but also it is very challenging to motivate them to take a significant role in the spiritual education of youths. And yet, youth pastors must seek help from parents and teachers because their roles are critical in youth ministry. For part-time youth pastors, this third standard is an extra burden. They may, however, address this need to the senior pastor. In this way, the senior pastor can be also a part of the youth ministry.

STANDARD FOUR
ASSESSING AND APPLYNG YOUTHS' FAITH LEARNING IN THEIR LIVES
(SOCIALLY-TRANSFORMATIVE TEACHING)

Objective: Youth pastors establish and clearly communicate learning goals for every teaching time in youth ministry (including small group Bible study, youth retreats, lock-ins, and other activities) for all youth members. Youth pastors ensure that the goals for each activity reflect the key themes of the Bible and theology. Based on the kingdom message of Jesus Christ, youth pastors encourage youth members to live their lives as light and salt of this world to seek peace and justice. Youth pastors use a variety of youth activities to plan and adjust learning opportunities that promote a deeper relationship with God and socially transformative living. Youth pastors further encourage youth members to become disciples of Christ by living their lives worthy of the gospel of Jesus Christ.

Key Questions to Ask: As youth pastors develop, they should ask, "How or why do I..."

1) involve all youth members and families in establishing justice through their daily lives?
2) work with other pastors (in and out of one's church) to establish similar teaching goals that promote socially-transformative living?
3) use a variety of activities (group or individual sharing, Bible study classes, mission trips, prayer walks, etc.) to determine what youth members know and are able to do?
4) develop and use tools and guidelines (Q.T. books, devotional books, etc.) that help all youth members to evaluate their lives during the weekdays?
5) help all youth members to develop a strong prayer life to listen carefully to God and discern wisely about their choices?
6) provide opportunities for all youth members to share their spiritual journey with others?
7) initiate and maintain regular contact with youth members about their daily struggles and joys?

It is often extremely difficult to assess youth members' knowledge about the Bible and Christian theology, and about their spiritual journey based on their learning. Unlike the school where teachers can just give exams to check students' knowledge, the church cannot evaluate youth members' theological learning with exams. The goal of this standard, therefore, is not to grade a youth member's spiritual life, but to promote, encourage, and inspire youth members to follow Christ and seek justice through God's love. By justice, I mean, to establish a right relationship. Youth members need to set a daily goal to seek justice, establish a right relationship with God first and then with others around them in everyday life.

STANDARD FIVE
CREATING AND MAINTAINING EFFECTIVE ENVIRONMENTS
FOR THE COMMUNITY OF JESUS CHRIST
(COMMUNALLY-ORIENTED TEACHING)

Objective: Youth pastors create a physical environment (worship room, Bible study rooms, and other spaces) as well as group dynamics that engage all youth members to be a community of Jesus Christ. Youth pastors encourage all youth members to participate in building up the community of Christ by working independently and collaboratively. Expectations for youth members' behavior as members of the body of Jesus Christ are established early, clearly understood, and consistently maintained. Youth pastors maintain safe youth group environments in which all youth members are treated fairly and respectfully. At the same time, youth members treat one another fairly and respectfully as brothers and sisters in Christ. Youth pastors use every youth activity to reinforce the importance of communally-oriented living.

Key Questions to Ask: As youth pastors develop, they should ask, "How or why do I..."

1) arrange the worship room and the Bible study room to facilitate positive communal interactions?
2) pace and adjust youth activities so that youth members remain engaged as one body of Christ?
3) involve all youth members, including newcomers, in the development of a faith community where all members feel welcomed and unified?
4) encourage youth members to bear and share the fruits of the Holy Spirit (love, joy, peace, patience, kindness, goodness, faithfulness, gentleness, and self-control) with one another to build up the community of Jesus Christ?
5) help all youth members accept and respect different experiences, ideas, backgrounds, feelings, and perspectives among the group?
6) invite all youth members to solve community-related problems and resolve conflicts through prayer and worship?
7) teach the theological meaning of a communally-oriented life for Christians?

Creating and maintaining unity in a youth group is every pastor's common hope. The goal of this standard, however, is not to simply promote unity, but to promote the theological meaning of the communal life of Christians as the body of Christ.

STANDARD SIX
DEVELOPING AS A JEONG-SHARING EDUCATOR/TEACHER/COUNSELOR/PASTOR
(JEONG-BASED TEACHING)

Objective: Youth pastors reflect on their ministry with the eyes of *jeong* and actively engage in sharing and teaching about *jeong*. Youth pastors establish *woo-jeong* between youth members themselves and between youth members and youth pastors through various activities. Youth pastors develop sincere *ae-jeong* towards the ministry and youth members. Youth pastors communicate effectively with youth members and their families about the role of *jeong* in youth ministry and involve everyone to become *jeong*-sharer as well in the community of faith. Youth pastors teach the theological meaning of *mo-jeong* to all youth members and why it is essential for *jeong*-based youth ministry.

Key Questions to Ask: As youth pastors develop, they may ask, "How or why do I…"

1) share *jeong* with others in the midst of a busy daily schedule?
2) continue to seek out and refine *jeong* approaches that make faith-teaching more meaningful to every youth members?
3) expand my knowledge about the profound meaning of *jeong* through the first generation Korean parents so they may share their *jeong* with me?
4) provide my youth members with *jeong*-based experiences that demand the radical understanding of the community of Christ?
5) promote positive dialogue and interactions with all youth members about the concept and practice of *jeong* in their youth community?
6) provide opportunities for all youth members to build *woo-jeong* and to understand and experience the profound *mo-jeong* of God?
7) maintain and practice my *ae-jeong* toward the youth ministry or youth members?

Building a deeper *jeong* between people cannot be done unless one spends a reasonable amount of time with the other. The quantity time matters more than the quality of time in the realm of *jeong*. Youth pastors who strive to share *jeong*, therefore, need to be available to spend extra time besides their assigned or "contracted" time in a youth group. Becoming a *jeong*-sharing pastor is more than being a good pastor because *jeong* is one of the highest valued characteristics in Korean community. Many first generation parents expect pastors to be full of *jeong* in their church. One of the worst evaluations of any pastor in a KA church context can receive is the lack of *jeong* in a pastor's heart. Pastors in KA churches can be substandard in preaching, teaching, or organizing skills, but cannot lack *jeong*.

The questions and characteristics of the MSYM have some overlaps between and among them. These overlaps are unavoidable since the interrelationships and complexities of faith education are evident in youth ministry. Again, the questions that I have posed in each standard must not be used as checklists to become the most effective youth pastor. Rather, I challenge youth pastors to change and add more reflective and developing questions throughout their journey of youth ministry.

Teaching Tools
The First Days of Youth Ministry

Kevin Ryan, author of *The Induction of New Teachers*, provides a helpful teaching progress model called, "The Four Stages of Teaching."[79] The four stages are 1) fantasy, 2) survival, 3) mastery, and 4) impact. The title of each stage explains its function well. The first stage reflects all first-year-teachers' enthusiastic yet naïve dream of becoming the best teacher ever to all the students in the class. Soon the reality of the students' level of understanding, heavy workloads, and work-related stress leads them to move on to the second stage, survival. In this stage, teaching becomes no more than a job. Teachers barely make it through the day, and do so just to survive. Harry Wong suggests that most teachers do not progress beyond this stage. The mastery stage is for those teachers who know how to manage their classroom well by teaching for mastery and having high expectations for their students. Only a few public school teachers reach the last stage of impact, where the teacher impacts not only students' knowledge but their lives as well. I see the similar pattern of stages for many first year youth pastors. In the following I set out a youth pastors' version of the Four Stages of Teaching:

---

[79] Kevin Ryan, *The Induction of New Teachers*, 1986.

The Four Stages of *Jundosa*

1. FANTASY – Most of the first-year seminarians who jump into children or youth ministry believe that they can bring revival to their new ministry location. They are very excited to be called "Jundo-sah-neem" (a title for pastors who are in process of ordination) and they are eager to preach and provide the best worship experience for all members. Based on their own past wonderful youth group experiences, they are in a fantasy stage of making their first ministry as successful as they can.

2. SURVIVAL – After the honeymoon period of being a new pastor to children or youth ends, they begin to realize that they have too much work to do. Lack of support and unbearable amount of church work begin to cause stress for the new passionate pastors. For those who are full time students at seminary, they begin to change their ministry attitude to a "survival" mode. Their ministry now becomes more like a "part-time" job or a fulfillment of the field-education requirement.

3. MASTERY – This stage is possible for those pastors who know how to manage and balance their ministry. Worship and preaching are well established. Many administrative tasks are properly organized. They preach and teach to make a difference and exhibit accountability with other youth workers.

4. IMPACT – Effective pastors are now impacting their children or youth members through preaching and other activities. Their goals and visions of ministry are clear and well communicated to youth members, parents, and volunteer teachers. The Lord's Day worship service is well organized and a pastor is eager to preach the good news to the youth members. Through youth pastor's passionate heart and "sticky" relationship of *jeong*, youth members begin to open up more to their pastors and enjoy learning from their pastor.

It is very difficult to move beyond the second stage, especially with a part-time status for many KA youth pastors. Although it is difficult to move on to the next stage, youth pastors have a reason to transcend the second stage: our calling is more than a "part-time job." It has to be done because youth pastors are teaching the Word of God, and it can be done because our strength comes from "the LORD, the Maker of heaven and earth" (Psalm 121:2).

Beside "trusting the LORD with all our hearts and lean not on [our] own understanding" (Prov. 3:5), the basic teaching and discipline tools of Wong and Wong can be used as excellent guidelines. After explaining why youth pastors need to succeed on the first days (or weeks) of ministries, I will briefly introduce some of the helpful teaching and discipline tips (out of many others) from Wong and Wong book.

Why Care About the First Days of Ministry?

Based on their teaching experiences and educational research, Harry and Rosemary Wong conclude that the first days of school are so critical that it can make or break the teacher.[80] The authors continue, "student achievement at the end of the year is directly related to the degree to which the teacher establishes good control of the classroom procedures in the very first week of the school year."[81] For this reason, the new teacher must have everything ready when school begins. To emphasize the importance of the first day, Wong and Wong even say that the teacher's "success during the school year will be determined by what [he/she does] on the first days of school.[82] I do not believe that is necessarily true in a youth ministry context, but the value of the first days of ministry is unquestionable: the first days of ministry can make or break the pastor. Youth pastors must be ready to preach and teach the Word of God in the very first days of ministry.

---

[80] Wong and Wong, 3.
[81] Ibid., 4.
[82] Ibid., 4.

Youth pastors must remember that they are hired to preach the gospel, not to please the youth members.[83]

To be an effective teacher for the first week of school, the authors suggest knowing at least three things: "1) what you are doing, 2) your classroom procedures, and 3) your professional responsibilities."[84] For youth pastors, the same three categories must be mastered before they begin their first days of ministry.

Efficient vs. Effective Pastor

> We are seeking a full-time [or part-time] youth pastor who can lead our youth ministry of 50 students. Duties include: preaching on Sundays and leading weekly programs, Bible study, summer missions, retreats, teacher training/recruiting, and activities.[85]

This is a typical youth pastor's job description for Korean American churches. The expectations are very high. Many

---

[83] Wong and Wong offer a challenging statement to first year teachers in the first page of his first chapter. The title of the statement is "Looking for Fun? Go to a Party." Wong and Wong write, "Douglas Brooks observed a group of teachers in his research. The most ineffective one were those who began the first day of school with an activity. Neophyte teachers, especially, can't wait to begin the first day of school with a fun activity. Please don't... Education should be challenging, exciting, engrossing, and thought-provoking, but not fun. If you want fun, go to a party, the beach, or a movie, go shopping, or take a vacation. If you believe that learning should be fun, you are doing the students a disservice. The student becomes a victim, thinking that everything in life should be fun and that anything that isn't fun is boring. School is a serious place. You go to school to study, work, and produce-just like an adult workplace. School is where you go to learn skills that help make you a productive citizen and grow to your fullest potential as a human being." The church context is very different, but the statement speaks clearly to youth pastors as well. The major concern for all youth pastors should be how to boldly preach and teach the Word of God, not how to make the youth group a fun place. Once youth pastors forget their main role (preacher), the whole youth ministry will fall apart.
[84] Wong and Wong, 4.
[85] Youth ministry job description from Korean Central Presbyterian Church of Houston (http://www.kamr.org/openings/sponsored).

churches expect youth pastors to be not only good preachers, but teenage counselors, administrators, worship leaders, missionaries, teacher's trainers and recruiters, and activity coordinators. All these roles are expected from a youth pastor as soon as he or she steps into the church. At the same time, almost all youth pastors are trying to fulfill these expectations from the very first days of ministry. Youth pastors at this fantasy stage, however, find themselves in the survival stage with "Things to do" lists as weeks pass by.

For this reason, youth pastors need to be an effective pastor rather than an efficient pastor. Harry and Rosemary Wong offer a helpful difference between becoming an effective teacher and an efficient teacher. The authors define *Efficient* as doing things right, and *Effective* as doing the right thing.[86] I have seen many youth pastors who try to do everything right (efficient pastors) rather than to do the right thing (effective pastors). With so many responsibilities and expectations, youth pastors often have no choice but to do everything correctly. But by spending too much energy and time on various assignments, youth pastors often forget to do the "right thing," namely, preaching the Word of God. Effective pastors preach the gospel and preach it well. Seminary preaching professors have taught me to spend at least one hour for every minute of my sermon. The preaching moment deserves at least that much time of preparation. The foremost "right thing" for youth pastors is preparing the sermon and preaching it well. The rest of the youth ministry related programs can be done either by teachers or youth members. Preaching, however, must be handled sincerely and diligently by youth pastors. Effective youth pastors spend the most amounts of time and energy on weekly sermons.

For this reason, youth group volunteer teachers and/or deacons and elders may be encouraged to take charge of planning retreats or other activities. Furthermore, youth members can initiate other activities as well. Many of the youth members are gifted in so many ways but often neglect their ability to participate in the ministry planning. Through the preaching moments, youth

---

[86] Wong & Wong, 5.

pastors need to challenge and inspire both teachers and youth members to participate in their youth ministry. One must be an effective youth pastor, rather than an efficient burnout.

Procedure and Routine

Classroom procedure and routine are extremely critical for teachers because they offer security to students. Since the serious business of learning does not come under insecure class settings, such security is crucial to many students. As Wong and Wong correctly argue, "students need to know from the very beginning how they are expected to behave and work in a classroom work environment." [87] In short, procedure means "what the teacher wants done," and routine means "what the students do automatically."[88] Although it is much more difficult to establish procedure and routine in a church setting, youth pastors must learn to use them in their teaching settings. I see at least two areas in any youth ministry setting where the procedures and routine can be easily implemented: the Lord's Day worship and the Bible study class.

The worship procedure can be clearly stated in a weekly bulletin so youth members can know what to expect on each Lord's Day worship service. The bulletin tells a youth member how elements of worship operate during the worship service. It does not only communicate the order of worship, but also what the pastor wants and expects from youth members during the worship services. For example, youth members are expected to sit quietly before the call to worship or they are expected to stand up during the praise time, etc. By clearly establishing the worship procedure, youth members know what they need to do in each order of worship. The worship procedure further offers security for the newcomers during the worship time. For the newcomers (both Christians and non-Christian youth), the clear worship procedure in

---

[87] Wong & Wong, 170.
[88] Ibid. 170.

the bulletin can greatly reduce new comers' anxiety during the worship services.

The regular worship procedure develops a routine for youth members. Wong and Wong define routine as "what the student does automatically without prompting or supervision. Thus a routine becomes a habit, practice, or custom for the student."[89] For many Christian traditions, the word "routine" has a negative connotation of doing something repeatedly without sincerity. To some it could be viewed as making youth members repeat their faith practice without any meaning in their lives. The routine that I and the public school education system suggest is not a meaningless repetition, but "habit, practice, or custom" for better learning. For example, a routine that I would like to establish for my youth group members on the Lord's Day morning is, as they come into the worship place, they sit quietly and pray for the preparation of worship. The bulletin would suggest the preparation prayer for worship every Lord's Day service and the youth will follow such instruction without prompting or supervision. Once the procedure of worship and a routine for a worshipper have been established, both youth pastor and youth members feel much more secure in their places, knowing what to do without any instruction.

For Bible study classes, a similar pattern is recommended. Youth members are less likely to be frustrated with clear classroom procedures. Such clarity allows more focused learning for youth members and, at the same time, it greatly reduces classroom disruptions. I always start the Bible study class with a sharing time where students share their lives with the class. Because of this opening procedure for every week, students know what to expect when they come to the class. Both procedure and routine build and offer a secure learning environment for youth members and teachers.[90]

---

[89] Wong & Wong, 170.
[90] See appendix B for a sample Bible study lesson plan.

Professional Responsibilities

Although the word "professional" sounds theologically problematic to many youth pastors, the lesson from the teacher's professionalism is worth noting. Throughout my teaching credential training courses, I have been taught to act and live like a "noble" teacher. Whether I am in the classroom or out in a shopping area, I have been told to behave like a noble teacher because my "actions and ethics convey meaning and hope to young people who look to [me] for guidance and example."[91] I was a professional math teacher who was not only expected to teach math, but to teach the value of education and life. I wonder whether youth pastors have a similar "professional" mind in their vocation. Some of the basic professional responsibilities of a youth pastor in the KA church are necessary to remember.

First, similar to public school teachers, youth pastors are in a helping profession. Youth pastors are not in private practice where we can work according to our own schedule. Wong and Wong speak clearly about this matter:

> Teaching is a craft. It is a service profession. If you want to choose your own hours, decide when and what you want to do, treat people as you please, create materials and keep them private, and avoid sharing and exchanging materials—go into private practice... Teachers are in the profession of helping people enhance the quality of their lives.[92]

Such a statement not only reminds the teachers which profession they are in, but also inspires them to live up to such a standard of living. Youth pastors, I believe, are also in a noble profession since we are not only trying to help people "enhance the quality of their lives," but to witness to the Creator who offers that very quality of

---

[91] Wong & Wong, vi.
[92] Ibid., 21.

their lives. Moreover, youth pastors are in their profession because of the calling of God. Youth pastors are the people who live their lives worthy to the gospel of Jesus Christ. The Lord Jesus Christ clearly did not choose his own hours, decide when he wanted to do something, treat people as he pleased, and create material and keep them private. Youth pastors are responsible to remember that we are in a helping profession for the sake of the gospel.

Since youth pastors are in a helping profession, I encourage youth pastors to act wisely with authorities of the church. I have witnessed too many unfortunate situations between first and the second generation church pastors. Many of the second generation youth pastors complain about "theological differences" between them and the first generation KA senior pastors or elders. As a 1.5 generation KA who grew up in a KA church, I see problems with both generations. Some of them are valid, some are not. To me, it is more a cultural or communication problem than a theological issue. No matter what the problem or difference is, however, as long as the church authorities allow youth pastors to preach the gospel of Jesus Christ, we must carry on our calling. Of course, there are many problems, just like any other churches, that the KA churches must engage and solve. Nonetheless, youth pastors should be thankful for allowing us to preach the gospel to many youth members in a church setting. Many youth pastors often forget that we are hired by God, first of all, and then by the Sr. pastor or the session. If we want to do everything our own way, we should go and plant a church. Unless God has called us to plant another church, we must support the Sr. pastor's ministry by continuing to proclaim the gospel of Jesus Christ to youth.

Secondly, we are responsible for how we dress. It is common sense for any profession that people will be treated as they are dressed. Of course God sees our heart, not our physical appearances. Unfortunately, we have only one God. The rest of the church members, including the parents and youth members, see our physical appearance before our heart. According to Wong's research, "the clothing worn by teachers affects the work, attitude, and discipline of students."[93] Wong and Wong argue that we dress for four main effects: 1) respect, 2) credibility, 3) acceptance, and 4) authority.[94] When a teacher has these four traits, the authors argue, the teacher has a much greater chance of influencing young people in their learning. Youth pastors in a church context, especially during the Lord's Day worship services, need to dress appropriately for such traits as well. Today's young people notice how their youth pastors are dressed. One's "clothing may not make a person, but it can be a contributing factor in unmaking a person."[95]

The way in which a youth pastor is dressed can offer a youth pastor a teaching moment as well. One of my education professors suggested that if one of my students asked me why I was dressed well all the time at school, to tell the student that "this is the way I express my respect to you." Youth pastors do not gain respect, credibility, acceptance, or authority by dressing up like a teenager during the Lord's Day worship services. We dress appropriately during the worship services to express our respect to youth members as well as to God.

Thirdly, youth pastors are responsible to be servant leaders of the youth ministry rather than workers. Wong and Wong offer helpful difference between workers and leaders,

A WORKER is concerned with time and money.
A LEADER is concerned with enhancement and cooperation.
A WORKER has a job
A LEADER has a career.
A WORKER is hired to do a job.
A LEADER is hired to think, make decisions, and solve problems.
A WORKER is an hourly laborer with a skill.
A LEADER is a professional with talent.
A WORKER can be fired from a job.
A LEADER cannot be fired from a career.[96]

---

[93] Wong and Wong, 55.
[94] Ibid., 55.
[95] Ibid., 55.
[96] Wong & Wong, 275. See the appendix for more characteristics of workers and leaders.

Obviously, becoming a leader rather than a worker is the goal for any teaching profession. As youth pastors, however, we are responsible for not only becoming a leader rather than a worker, but becoming a faithful servant leader of Jesus Christ. Youth pastors are responsible for being a leader by serving youth members, "for even the Son of Man did not come to be served, but to serve, and to give his life as a ransom for many" (Mark 10:45).

Moving Beyond the Survival Stage

Skipping the survival stage and moving onto the third or fourth stage of teaching is not the goal of the first year youth pastor. It takes many years of youth ministry experience and the grace of God to move beyond the second stage of survival. The good news is, however, that the gospel of Jesus Christ can be proclaimed in any stage of teaching that we are currently in. Even if we do not have any professional standards or teaching tools and experiences, the Holy Spirit can use us to proclaim the gospel if we are available. The goal of the MSYP and the teaching and disciplining tools of Wong and Wong is, therefore, to equip us to be effective youth pastors so we can be ready to proclaim the gospel when the Holy Spirit stirs our passion. Youth pastors must be ready to preach. While we are waiting to preach, we can prepare ourselves to be a better preacher and teacher using the MSYP and the first days of ministry teaching tools.

All six standards of MSYP offer evaluation criteria for a youth pastors' own teaching and preaching performances. Through an honest evaluation, youth pastors can improve youth ministry to be more faithful to the gospel. The first days of ministry teaching tools (knowing what you are doing, your classroom procedures, and your professional responsibilities) further equip youth pastors to be ready for the gospel moments. The three most importance words to a teacher, according to Wong and Wong, are "preparation, preparation, preparation."[97] The three most importance words to a

---

[97] Wong & Wong, 94.

youth pastor, from my experience, are praying, preparation, and preaching. Let us pray and prepare ourselves well, so we can boldly preach the gospel to our youth.

CHAPTER SIX

CONCLUSION
IN THE END... GOD

What I envy the most about Moses is his intimate relationship with God. In Deuteronomy 34:10, Moses is known as the one who "knew the LORD face to face." The first description of Moses from the later generations is about his profound relationship with God. The Hebrew word "to know" denotes an intimate relationship throughout the Old Testament. According to Olson, however, knowing God "face to face," pushes the level of intimacy even higher, straining to express near equality.[98] Indeed, God did speak to Moses "face to face, as one speaks to a friend" (Exod. 33:11). For the future generations after Moses, his deep and intimate relationship with God is valued the most at the end of Deuteronomy. I wonder how I will be evaluated by my future generations. The most passionate youth pastor ever? The best youth preacher ever? or The most effective youth pastor who was full of *jeong*? Well, I don't know. But I sincerely hope that my youth members will be able to remember me as the one who had an intimate relationship with God. More than anything in my

---

[98] Olson, 169.

career, I truly hope to speak to God "face to face, as one speaks to a friend" every moment of my life.

I hope and pray that other youth pastors also desire foremost to have such a relationship with God. Our theological and educational knowledge can make us arrogant scholars. Specialized youth ministry approaches or methods can also make us prideful youth workers. But only a deep relationship with God and the experience of God's grace and love make us humble youth pastors like Moses who was "a very humble man, more humble than anyone else on the face of the earth" (Num. 12:3). Any knowledge about youth ministry must be soaked in the grace of God. Martin Luther summarizes the point well:

> Therefore we are nothing, even with all our great gifts, unless God is present. When He deserts us and leaves us to our own resources, our wisdom and knowledge are nothing. Unless He sustains us continually, the highest learning and even theology are useless.[99]

Without a true relationship with God, everything that we do is meaningless. Without the presence of God in our lives, we are only a resounding gong or a clanging cymbal to our youth members. As a gardener who cultivates the garden according to the Owner's way, it makes sense to have a good relationship with the Owner.

In order to be a faithful cultivator of organic faith for the younger generations in a KA context, I have suggested the Five Deuteronomic Ministry Principles of Moses and the concept and practice of *jeong* as theological tools. For practical tools, I proposed the Ministry Standards for Youth Pastors and the three teaching tools for the first days of ministry. These cultivating tools do not guarantee the production of organic faith for the next generation. But that is not our goal, anyway. The goal of using any tools for God's garden is not to produce but to faithfully cultivate.

---

[99] Luther, 114.

At the end of his amazing career, Moses offers a final prayer and blessing for the younger generation. After all that he has done, Moses lays down his ministry and life to trust God to carry on what God has initially started with God's people. Olson suggests that such an "act of prayer is a confession of human limitations."[100] I believe the act of prayer is also a confession of human *jeong*. As much as *woo-jeong* and *ae-jeong* help youth pastors to have sticky staying power with youth and youth ministry, it is God's *mo-jeong* that binds us all, helps us to lay our ministries and lives and trust in God to carry on what God has started in us. In God's everlasting *mo-jeong*, we must never stop praying for our youth. Just like Christ never ceases to pray for all of us, let us never cease to pray for our youth members and their families until we literally see God face to face.

> The Lord bless you and watch, guard, and keep you;
> The Lord make His face to shine upon and enlighten you
> and be gracious (kind, merciful, and giving favor) to you;
> The Lord lift up His [approving] countenance upon you
> and give you peace (tranquility of heart and life continually).
>
> (Numbers 6:24-26, AMP)

---

[100] Olson, 160.

Bibliography

Anderson, Bernhard W. *Understanding the Old Testament*. Upper Saddle River, NJ: Prentice-Hall, 1998.

Bonhoeffer, Dietrich. *Life Together*. New York, Harper and Brothers: 1954.Brueggemann, Walter, *The Creative Word: Canon as a Model for Biblical Education* Philadelphia: Fortress, 1982.

Dean, Kenda C. *Practicing Passion: Youth and the Quest for a Passionate Church*. Grand Rapids: Eerdmans, 2004.

Eckardt, Burnell F. "Luther and Moltmann: The Theology of the Cross," *Concordia Theological Quarterly* 49 (1985): 19.

Forde, Gerhard. *On Being a Theologian of the Cross: Reflections on Luther's Heidelberg Disputation, 1518*. Grand Rapids, Michigan: Eerdmans Publishing Co., 1997.

Fretheim, Terrance E. *The Pentateuch*. Nashville: Abingdon Press, 1996.
Hall, Douglas J. "Luther's Theology of the Cross," *Consensus* 15 (1989): 7-19.

_____. "The Theology of the Cross for Our Day," Lutheran, (March, 2004).

Hurh, Won-Moo. *The Korean Americans*. Westport, CT: Greenwood Press, 1998.

Joh, Wonhee Anne, *Heart of the Cross: A Postcolonial Christology*, (Louisville, Kentucky: Westminster John Knox Press, 2006),

Kim, In-su. *Han'guk Kidok kyohoe ui yoksa (The History of Korean Church)*. Seoul: Changnohoe Sinhak Taehakkyo Ch'ulp'anbu: Presbyterian Theological Seminary Press, 1997.

Kwon, H., Kim, K., and Warner R. S., ed. *Korean Americans and Their Religions: Pilgrims and Missionaries from a Different Shore*. University Park, Pennsylvania: The Pennsylvania State University Press, 2001.

Kysar, Robert. *Stumbling in the Light: New Testament Images for a Changing Church.* St. Louis: Chalice Press, 1999.

Lee, Inn Sook and Timothy Son. *Asian Americans and Christian Ministry.* Seoul: Voice Publishing House, 1999.

Lee, Sang Hyun and John V. Moore, eds. *Korean American Ministry: A Resource Book.* Louisville, KY: Presbyterian Church (USA), 1993.

Luther, Martin. *Luther's Works,* American Edition, vols. 26: *Lectures on Galatians I,* ed. St. Louis: Concordia, 1963.

May, Scottie et. al. *Children Matter: Celebrating Their Place in the Church, Family, and Community.* Grand Rapids: Eerdmans, 2005.

Miller, Patrick D., *Deuteronomy: Interpretation, A Bible commentary for teaching and preaching.* Louisville: John Knox Press, 1990.

Moltmann, Jurgen, *Experiences in Theology.* London : SCM Press, 2000.

_____. *The Crucified God,* tr.R.A. Wilson and John Bowden [from the German *Der gekreuzigte Gott,* published by Christian Kaiser Veriag, Munich, second ed., 1973]. New York: Harper and Row, 1974.

_____. *In the End-The beginning: The Life of Hope*, Trans. Margaret Kohl Minneapolis: Fortress Press, 2004.

Niebuhr, H. Richard. *The Responsible Self.* New York: Harper & Row, 1963.

Nouwen, Henri. *The Road to Daybreak: A Spiritual Journey.* New York: Doubleday, 1988.

Olson, Dennis T. *Deuteronomy and the Death of Moses.* Minneapolis: Fortress Press: 1994.

Presbyterian Church (U.S.A.). *The constitution of the Presbyterian Church (U.S.A.) : Part I, Book of confessions.* New York, N.Y. : Offices of the General Assembly, 1981.

Roof , Wade C. *Spiritual Marketplace : baby boomers and the remaking of American religion.* Princeton, N.J. : Princeton University Press, 1999.

Root, Andrew. "Reexamining Relational Youth Ministry: Implications from the Theology of Bonhoeffer," *Word and World* volume 26, Number 3, (summer 2006): 270.

Ryan, Kevin. *The Induction of New Teachers*. Bloomington, Indiana: Phi Delta Kappa, 1986.

Sakenfeld, Katharine D. *The Meaning of Hesed in the Hebrew Bible: A New Inquiry* Missoula: Scholars Press, 1978.

Smith, Christian. *Soul Searching: The Religious and Spiritual Lives of American Teenagers*. Oxford: Oxford University Press, 2005.

Strommen, Merton P. and Hardel, Richard A. *Passing on the Faith: A radical New Model for Youth and Family Ministry*. Winona, MN: Saint Mary's Press, 2000.

Taffel, Ron. *Breaking Through To Teens: A New Psychotherapy for the New Adolescence*. NY: Te Guilford Press, 2005.

Wong, H., Wong, R., *The First Day of School: How to be an Effective Teacher*. Mountain View, CA: Harry K. Wong Publications, 1998.

Yeago, David S. "'A Christian, Holy People': Martin Luther on Salvation and the Church," *Modern Theology* 13 (1997): 101-120.

Yoo, B.W. *Korean Pentecostalism: Its History and Theology*. New York: Verlag Peter Lang, 1987.

TASTE THE YOUTH MINISTRY

i HOPE 아이홉

Cover photograph: Mimi Lee, 9th grade

www.ingramcontent.com/pod-product-compliance
Lightning Source LLC
LaVergne TN
LVHW051701080426
835511LV00017B/2671